Wealth
Increasing
Now

Gaining Assets, Managing Effectively

Using practical approaches to develop your Wealth consciousness and the basic traits to accumulate Wealth

Robert N. Wilson

Atlanta, Georgia, USA

Forward by Professor C.W. Copeland, Ph.D.

ISBN 978-0-9721065-2-8

Printed in the United States of America.

Preface

Why did I write this book titled "WIN" (Wealth Increasing Now)? Well, let me start by saying that this book was written to instruct on how to retire and experience financial freedom. To make my case, please indulge me as I provide you with a few facts.

First, let me say that I am not promoting retirement as you may currently know it. My reference to it is to keep this as simple as possible.

In 1997, the American Association of Retired Persons (AARP) started asking people at what age they planned to retire. The response was mid to late sixties. In the latest survey, almost half of the respondents said they plan to work into their seventies or beyond. Although the need for money is a driving force, some people would continue to work even if they didn't need the money.

This book is intended to be the follow-up to my book "Unlocking Wealth." Its whole purpose is to continue teaching the process of what it will take to build wealth.

The foundation that I laid in my last book should be solid enough for you to begin to build WEALTH. Regardless of your age or income, the steps that I hope you will learn have worked for many years.

Let me assure you that this book is not about failure, nor is it about making mistakes. It is simply about learning how having all of your eggs in one basket can make a difference in building wealth.

While writing this book, I was in the middle of conducting a number of personal makeovers on families at my very first financial retreat.

During my research period of figuring out what would be the best master plan to place with these families to reach financial independence, I discovered that wealth accumulation sounds complicated, but it is actually very simple. It's so simple that I want to give you a process that you can learn and implement in your life now.

As you move forward in this book, I want you to have a spirit of readiness and be willing to accept the simple. It will be so easy to make this more complicated than what it should be.

However, if you just started with this book, you may find that without learning sound money principles and how to manage your money, you may be just spinning your wheels. Having the right foundation and commitment will make all of the difference in the world.

I am sure that this book will make an impact on your life like nothing else has before. After many hours of tinkering with many families' financial situations, I believe that we have put together a solid plan for you. Please read this entire book carefully and prepare to enjoy a new financial experience.

Most of us, if not all of us, have this erroneous idea about how wealth is accumulated, or we have no real idea at all. Our parents were not able to teach what wealth is or how to create it.

In fact, I remember things like saving for rainy days simply meant to keep some money in a jar or box hidden somewhere in the house.

There was never more than $100 at a time, if that much. Yet, many, if not all of the things that I will talk about, were available at that time. As important as this subject of accumulating wealth is, we were not taught about it.

We all have lived a portion of our lives watching television and movies that have created the best images of what wealth might be. Yet, it seems so distant from us and so unreal.

As I try to guide you through the book to learn more about how wealth is accumulated, it is also so important that we remember how much we really do not know.

Many people have a limited perspective and suspect that wealthy individuals have obtained their wealth through some financial masterstroke, married into money, obtained it through inherited money or simply through luck.

This stroke of luck includes winning the lottery, getting into the "right" stock or business on the ground floor, or just being lucky enough to know the right people at the right time. They say timing is everything; we will talk about that later.

While any of these situations could surely jumpstart your wealth-building program, they are by no means typical of how most wealthy people become that way.

As a matter of fact, coming into lots of money quickly before learning how to manage it, can actually be hazardous to your wealth. That is why I refer back to the book, "Unlocking Wealth".

After being on the radio every day for more than ten years, I have learned that regardless of how much I preach budgeting or money management, many of my listeners still feel that they need more money to do what they want to do.

Even after hours and hours of educating them about the wealth accumulation process, they have not learned that simply finding more money seldom solves the problems.

As I stated in "Unlocking Wealth," many people, given more money, only get deeper into debt. There are so many stories of people who came into a windfall of some sort only to wind up right back where they started (or worse) because they never learned how to manage money.

Research has shown that it is rarely luck, inheritance, advanced degrees or even intelligence that enables people to build wealth. It is more often hard work, thorough planning, persistence and most of all self-discipline that gets the job done. I believe that almost everybody with a steady job can create a fortune of some kind.

We need only to get an education, a decent job, learn how to save and invest our money. Anyone can do it. You can do it, too!

I intend to show you how quickly your money can grow into wealth, why you must create a life plan and the basic elements of what the financial plan for your life should be.

I am going to teach financial freedom and wealth building in a way that will influence your family for generations to come.

It is unusual that a single financial occurrence will result in real wealth. For the vast majority of people, it comes about as the consequence of a master plan of saving and investing small but regular amounts of money over long periods of time on a systematic and consistent basis.

I have talked about it as it relates to developing a relationship with your money, now prepare yourself to gain a better understanding of how to "be about it." Remember, you have the power to WIN!

There is a **New Paradigm Shift** that I have discovered during my research for writing this book. There must be a shift in rediscovering your core financial desires. Understand, the rules of wealth are steadfast and require a complete shifting of your commitment to create wealth.

It is called **Action Influence. Action Influence** is simply taking the definition of paradigm and applying its meaning to influence your financial decision.

Those who recognize the shift adjust and focus on creating wealth for the next generation. (**Paradigm** - A set of assumptions, concepts, values and practices that constitutes a way of viewing reality for the community that shares them, especially in an intellectual discipline.)

Acknowledgements

In the course of writing this book, there were many moments when I had to dig deep inside and I would like to acknowledge what and whom I found there. There is GOD: the only thing greater than myself. His Grace and His Mercy have become more evident in my life.

In all of my years of knowing and reading the Word of God, He has now revealed Himself. To Him be all glory and honor for any wisdom that you may find in this book. Next, there are two powerful men of God, Bishop Victor P. Smith and Bishop Dale C. Bronner, my spiritual father and shepherd that were used by God to guide and encouraged me.

Then the wisdom of both of my beloved parents, each of them has left a mark within me that I cannot put into words. There is my wife Jennifer, my son Carlos, who constantly challenges me to be a great husband, father, a daddy and a friend.

And then as I looked deep inside of me, I found my friends: Guy and Lena, Peter and Janice, Daryl and Gail, Pamela, Tony, Mike, Milton, Steve, Brian, Franz, Marc, Gregory, Selena, Yolanda, Carol, and so many more; a part of each of them is within me.

They say you are what you eat, I have received something from each of them. Thank you all.

I would also like to extend my appreciation to those who have directly aided me in my business development and the publication of this book.

Nathaniel H. Bronner, Jr. who has been a mentor to me in business sharing his valuable knowledge. C. W. Copeland for teaching me the value of relationships. Dr. Chris Boyd who quietly persuaded me to move forward.

Marian Barnes with the incredible ability to listen with fairness. Also, Ron, Marian, Monica, Charles, Steve, Milton, Phyllis, Kathy, Shirley, George, Cathy, and Madeline.

Each of them has taught me patience in the final weeks of this book. But, most importantly they have tolerated me.

Wealth Increasing Now, requires a paradigm shift in every way, including relationships. I would like to thank Gwen Trahan for the sacrifices she made to jump right on this and meet the deadline.

Also, Wanda, Teresa, Allison, Marvin, and Martin for their input. Finally yet importantly, special thanks are due to many people in the radio industry that have provided me the chance to share great words of encouragement directly to the general public.

I could write a monster of a book, just about what all of my family, friends and business acquaintances really mean to me, but for now, I want to say **Thanks To You All.**

Forward

Robert Wilson is known for his passion for helping consumers make good financial decisions. Throughout his career he has taken a bold stance against "financial genocide". Few people in this industry are as dedicated to making a difference in the lives of others as Robert N. Wilson.

As an author, he has compiled a sensational list of books promoting financial freedom by understanding the premise of "Unlocking Wealth". The thing that impresses me the most about Mr. Wilson's writings is that he provides real-life examples for his readers and encourages them to become engaged in their own success.

As a radio personality, Mr. Wilson has been tagged with the moniker "The Credit Surgeon"; however, his level of financial knowledge is far broader than a single topic.

Although most people that remember him from the early 1990s, recall a former bill collector turned consumer advocate. Mr. Wilson has not changed his no-nonsense, in-your-face, consumer-gladiator style; but he has expanded the depth and breadth of his topics.

While his presence does loom large, it has been a pleasure to be affiliated with Mr. Wilson for nearly 20 years, because he is constantly developing innovative approaches to solving financial dilemmas.

His recent brain-buster is Action Influence, which is a paradigm-shifting strategy, which directs the consumer away from a poverty mentality to a wealth mentality.

Action Influence appears that it may become the next high-lighted concept of discussion among the thought of leaders in the Behavioral Economics community.

While Action Influence is the "franchise player" among a list of outstanding topics in Mr. Wilson's new book, *Wealth Increasing Now (W.I.N.)*, it has a few challengers for the title.

The list of topics is full and diverse; however, a common thread is that they empower the consumer to systematically self-review and self-correct their financial behavior.

I am looking forward to experiencing the wave of behavior change that is sure to happen with the release of *Wealth Increasing Now.* I expect that it will afford generations the opportunity to *W.I.N.*

C.W. Copeland, Ph.D.
Professor, The Huebner School
The American College of Financial Services

Contents

Chapter 1

How Is Wealth Really Accumulated?

How is wealth really accumulated? Great question! Let's start by saying it's simple. Having financial ETHICS is the fundamental step to achieving wealth. The patience and commitment these ETHICS require is the difficult part. What are financial *ETHICS*?

Effort Time Habit Investing Commit Saving

Effort is the biggest challenge. It requires you to focus, resist the temptation to overspend and take on unnecessary debt.
Time is needed in order to focus on developing a plan of action. You must realize the value time has on money.
Habit forming behavior is necessary to maintain consistency in managing money.
Investing time after time, month after month, in stocks, bonds and mutual funds.
Commit to having a financial vision for your future.
Saving every single penny, nickel, dime, quarter and dollar for the purpose of wealth creation.

There must be a mindset transformation. Before wealth can be accumulated, you must refocus on what you think you know about money.

It must become a conscious effort surrounded by financial ethics. Another way to look at it is simply having principles on how you manage every dollar that hits your hands.

Many people consider wealth as something evil. Society has created an image or perception that money is the ultimate test in our culture. Some have said, "If money is not the root of all evil, the absence of it is the source of guilt, anger and humiliation." I say that it's your mentality.

If you are not wealth-minded, the only other option is being poverty-minded. Knowing the difference between these two mentalities gives you the best chance of accumulating wealth.

The fact is that people who accumulate money tend to keep accumulating it. People who do not accumulate money lose even the little bit that they have. You must consider what you think about money. It shows you who you are and what you have.

This is beyond the movie star lifestyle as you see depicted in reality TV shows and movies. There is a real image of your mentality. You are either wealthy or prosperous: filling your mind with thoughts, words, and images of wealth, affluence, success, productivity and solutions the majority of the time.

Or, you have a poverty lack and failure mentality that signifies you aren't interested in knowing the consequences of your choices and actions.

So, again, how is wealth really accumulated? I will answer this in the best way possible. It is created. Yes, I said created.

Every dollar that you have possession of can start the process of creating wealth. Remember that being poverty-minded is the major factor that stops you from accumulating wealth and thinking positive in the terms of wealth accumulation.

Many people find themselves on jobs that seem to head no-where. Yet, money is being earned everyday that they show up for work.

I know people who really hate getting up every day going to a job that they do not like. The one driving force that keeps them getting up and returning day after day to this same job is to pay bills.

This mentality is very clear that having a job can be hazard-ous to your wealth. It is a working poor mentality. Just going to work a job to earn an income to pay bills is not enough.

Is much easier for them to desire and have the need for more money. Nevertheless, they find themselves creating more debt and obligations that must be paid. As a result, they are accumulating debt rather than wealth.

I hope to show that some of the same issues that would push you to create debt could be the used for creating wealth. Al-low me to compare creating debt and creating wealth.

We all have heard of the term compounding interest. Most of you understand what it is and how it works. Yet, it is not ap-plied to the principle of wealth creation.

When we go out and purchase items on credit or a delayed repayment plan, each time we are compounding debts and obligations on top of each other.

Let's take a person that recently purchased a new home. They now have the best reason possible to replace or purchase new items for the home. Most commonly, they are out of cash due to the process of buying the home.

Yet, they feel that they need new furniture, new appliances, new clothes and often times a new car. All of these things help make that person feel that they now have reached higher levels than they really are.

The fact is they have now compounded the amount of financial liabilities to a point that may become overwhelming.

Let's take a closer look.

Item Purchased	Cost
New Home	$350,000.00
New Furniture	$6,500.00
New Clothes	$2,000.00
New Car	$26,000.00
House Warming	$5,000.00
Debt Total	**$389,500.00**

Within possibly 90–120 days, a family can create debt as much as eight times their annual income. This is accumulation of the wrong things.

Before you begin to justify in your mind and heart that there is a difference here, let me define a few key points.

- **Compound Debt–unpaid debt that is added to the liabilities so that subsequent debt is calculated on the grossed-up amount.**
- **Compound Interest – unpaid interest that is added to the principal so that subsequent interest is calculated on the grossed-up amount.**
- **Accumulate – to heap or pile up.**

Now, we can look at it another way; a way that gives you a better opportunity to reach real financial goals. Do the math.

Start with one penny and double it every day. Within one month, the power of compounding will have made you over one million dollars.

Here is what you are doing. Each day you will double the previous day's amount. Continue to do that for 30 days. .01 + .01 is .02 .02 + .02 is .04, and so on.

It is only when we continue to add to our original amount that we start to see the miraculous nature of the power of compounding.
.04 + .04 is .08. (Day 3)
.08 + .08 is .16. (Day 4)
.16 + .16 is .32. (Day 5)

Unbelievably, by day 27 - yes day 27 - you will have accumulated **$1,342,177.20**. This is 100% compounding, it is the simplest way to show you the effect. You may never be able to compound at 100% each time, but it is the mentality of wealth that if it is only 10%, it is great stuff.

How will you harness the power of this great tool in your business? In taking immediate actions? In compounding your thoughts? In multiplying your results?

Before you dismiss this idea as impossible, why not try it? Just take it one step at a time. In chapter 10, you will see our **Action Influence** savings plans to help you start your savings goals. At what level of success does your mind start to insist that you can do it? Remember, your beliefs and attitudes give power to your actions.

I do not want to lose my focus here. Remember, it's about creating wealth that will come about by eliminating debt and accumulating assets. For many it may begin small with something as little as a penny.

How much wealth is really possible from saving small but regular amounts of money over long periods of time on a systematic and consistent basis?

I used Wachovia Bank (now Wells Fargo) for a product they had that I believe was so under used. It was called systematic savers. It was great for starting the process of saving money in regular amounts over long periods of time.

The program considered the age of a person and their minimum earning per year. The younger a person was increased their total earning capacity.

For example, if you have a basic income of $35,000 a year and you decide that you will use 10% to invest in three different types of products on a monthly basis; your projection could be well over $1.8 million by the time you retire.

The assumption would be that 6% goes into one product
while the other 4% would be equally divided into the two
remaining products. You will see a clearer process of this in
chapter 9.

If you are presently 30 years old and earning $35,000 per
year, your projection could be worth about $1.8 million by
the time you retire at age 65 if you follow the principles out-
lined in this book.

Based on your salary, and if your employer matches a portion of your contribution, there is a possibility that your
retirement could be worth even more. Assumptions will have
to be made based on your willingness to take sound and
committed action to influence the outcome.

Assuming that you contribute 2% to a regular account as
well would provide you with additional savings by age 65.
The three accounts would add up to more than $1.8 million.

Your totals would, of course, be higher if you earn more,
contribute more, work longer before retiring, or if your rate
of return proves to be higher than projected.

Keep in mind there is something called the rate of inflation
that will affect the overall dollar value at the time of retirement.

My goal is to show how that impact can be dealt with over
the life of your master plan. Once the proper adjustments are
made, you will be amazed at the wealth you will be able to
create. Time gives you the opportunity to maximize your results.

The most important variable in the compound interest equation is the variable of time. How *soon* you start to save money is *much* more important than how much you may be able to put away once you start.

Do not get caught up with the idea that you should put off saving money until you make more money. This is a major trap for most of the working class. They seem to feel that they need to earn more to save.

Start early because early money earns the most of any money, which is what compounding, is really all about. It's much more important to **start immediately** with even a few dollars a month than to wait until you can save a more meaningful amount later.

Most of you would not be surprised when I point out that the sooner you start your investment plan, the more money you will accumulate by retirement age.

This would seem to be simple mathematics: the longer you save, the more you will save. But many of you *may* be surprised by the *amount* of this difference.

An individual saving 12% of a $36,000 salary with a 3% company match would attain the following results by age 65 depending on their age when they started.

Age 29...$2,679,994
Age 32...$1,953,108
Age 35...$1,416,738
Age 38...$1,021,402
Age 41...$ 730,439

As you can see, there's more going on here than just simple mathematics. There's a compounding effect of money earning money on the money that earned money on the money, etc., with the result that "early money" earns much more than money put in later during the time period.

A 29-year-old individual would cost himself almost three-quarters of a million dollars by waiting three years to start his program. A 32-year-old individual would cost himself a half-million by waiting 3 years.

And the difference between starting at 29 and starting at 41 is nearly two million dollars. So, start to save now, give yourself a real chance of being able to have money during your retirement.

Another point needs to be made here as well. Your investment program is *not* going to stop at age 65 or 70 or any other pre-determined age just because you decide to retire.

You may stop making additional contributions after you retire or reach a certain age, but your accumulated balance is going to continue to grow. It could possibly even grow at a faster rate than you can take it out.

So add another 20 years or so of compounding to the results shown above, and you'll see even more clearly the importance of starting immediately. "Early money" will have an extra 20 years of earning power!

By now, I am sure you have come to understand that becoming wealthy and remaining that way is not very likely to "just happen." You have to have a solid plan!

Even if you expect to inherit money someday, marry into it, or win the lottery, you need to have a financial plan, because without one you are not likely to stay wealthy very long.

When you operate from a well-conceived financial plan, you can determine your destination and identify the routes you intend to follow to get there, just as you would if you were planning a trip.

You can know in advance how much progress you should expect to make in a given amount of time by using financial calculators, and you can gauge how well you are doing. It is important to see how you are progressing year to year with your savings.

The vast majority of people in this country, young or other-wise, do not operate from any sort of financial master plan at all. They pretty much fly by the seat of their pants, financial-ly speaking, reacting to events and emergencies as they occur, instead of taking control of their affairs and making things happen in accordance with *their* wishes, and in keep-ing with *their* set timetable.

As a result of this lack of financial planning, the majority of people in this country are not yet wealthy, which should tell you something: Do not be one of them. We have to develop a plan. Your plan should incorporate the following elements:

A) Take control (Create a budget)
B) Automatic investment (401k)
C) An ideal timing strategy (Set Goals)
D) Debt elimination (Get rid of the cancer)
E) Automatic savings (IRA's Annuities)
F) Automatic reinvestment (Compound)

How is wealth really accumulated?   Action Influence

In these next chapters, I want you to follow me as I elaborate on each of these elements. In turn, you will see how each of them should fit into your well-conceived master plan for building wealth.

A Motivational Quote

Begin to live your dream this very day. Dress like you would dress. Speak like you would speak. Walk like you would walk if the goal were already achieved. Practice the skills you will use when you have arrived at your goal.

Act as if it is yours. And soon it will be. See it clearly, specifically, to the point where your moment to moment life becomes your dream. When your life becomes your dream, then your dream will be a very real, lasting part of your life. You have GREATNESS within you!!

 - Les Brown is a dynamic personality and highly-sought-after renowned motivational speaker.

What you should have learned in this chapter:

1. Financial <u>ETHICS</u> are the fundamental steps to accumulating wealth.
2. There must be a transformation of your mindset.
3. Every dollar can start the process of creating wealth.
4. Being poverty-minded is one major factor that prevents wealth from accumulating.
5. Wealth is possible by saving small regular amounts of money over long periods of time on a consistent basis.
6. Compounding affects the money earning money on the money that earned money on the money you invested.
7. Success comes from a well-conceived financial plan.

Chapter 2

Taking Control – Getting Started

I want you to commit to creating a financial future for you and your family. I am going to challenge many of your preceded notions about money and how you deal with it. The goal is to lay a solid foundation for building and creating wealth for you and your family.

In order to complete this task, an open and focused mind will be needed. You will be given an assignment, but I would like for you to also push beyond your assignment.

Some of you may have taken courses in dealing with personal finance before. This, I trust, will be different for you. My approach is not complicated. Yet, it's simple and practical enough for the concepts to become clear to you.

As I show you principles in dealing with money, I want you to understand that the application can vary. By the end of this book, you will be able to walk away with real results that fit your lifestyle.

There will be information repeated throughout the book. The purpose of this is to put as much emphasis on the things that will help you take control.

Remember, as you read this book, take advantage of sharing your challenges and stories as it relates to every area that you uncover with your family.

Knowing your family is important in this process. The goal here will be to change the financial pattern of the next generation.

For some of you, what I'm sharing may seem simple. It may seem to be things you knew already. Granted, there may be things that you have tried and done, but please stay focused on learning new processes so that you may understand how to fully apply your new knowledge and reach your goals.

For you to be truly successful in life, you must first determine your goals. Learn to set long and short-term goals that fit into a master plan.

I want you to create your own step-by-step, customized plan. You should be able to prioritize and plan a budget; setting financial goals for the future to ensure that you efficiently utilize your money.

There are other areas that will have a direct affect on budgeting. They are: <u>Self-Awareness</u>, <u>Conscience</u>, <u>Creative Imagination</u>, and <u>Independent Will</u>.

Let's talk about each of these briefly:

Self-Awareness is when we know we need to do something. We know what, when, and how. Yet, we convert our self-awareness into selfishness. Selfishness is deciding this is what I want now, right or wrong.

Conscience is the internal guidance system. It allows us to sense when we act or even contemplate acting. We recognize the distinction between right and wrong in regard to our own conduct. Or, we choose to conform to our own sense of right conduct.

Creative Imagination is when we justify the things we do or not do. For instance, at Christmas time we will delay paying the light bill, telephone bill, cable bill, or some other bills to buy gifts. We will go deeper in debt, knowing that our financial situation cannot handle any more debt.

Independent Will allows us to really feel good about the decisions we make regardless of the outcome of our actions. It is the ability to act freely without any outside influence. It is the point where we stand our ground on all of our decisions.

You Must Budget (Wealth Conscious)

For many people, the word "budget" has a negative connotation. Instead of thinking of a budget as financial handcuffs, think of it as a means to achieve your highest financial success.

Whether you make thousands of dollars a year or hundreds of thousands of dollars a year, a budget is the first and most important step you can take towards putting your money to work for you instead of being controlled by it and forever falling short of your financial goals.

To those of you who think you know where your money goes without keeping detailed records, I issue this challenge:

keep track of every cent you spend for one month. I promise you'll be surprised and perhaps shocked by how much some of your "small" expenditures add up to.

Budgeting and establishing your expenses gives you a strong sense of where your money goes and can help you reach your financial goals, whether they are saving for a down-payment on a house, starting a college fund for your kids, buying a new car, planning for retirement, paying off the credit cards, or saving for that trip to Aruba.

Budgeting puts you on the road to wealth-consciousness. Yet, it may seem that you are more poverty-conscious be-cause of the stance you have to take. Without budgeting, financial matters become the source of discord.

The purpose here is getting a handle on your spending, im-plementing a budget, and saving for the future. This will create positive effects on your relationship with your partner or spouse as well as others.

Do you have control with what is going on with your mon-ey? If not, then you will need to focus here very closely. I know you have heard about budgeting over and over again. I find it confusing at times when I look at the many different types of budgets.

Let me try to simplify what a budget is. There are a number of words that come to mind right away.

Organization
Operation
Planning
Map

Each of these words can be associated with budgeting in some way. The dictionary describes a budget as a financial statement or financial plan. I want to use the word "Control" to describe how I prefer you to consider it.

By establishing financial control in your home, your family's organization is established. Your primary role in this organization is to create the control in which you will operate. There are basics that must be done regardless of what is happening outside or inside your organization.

Tithes and Offering. If your faith asks this of you, then it cannot be compromised. Mortgage or Rent. This expense is recurring every month and is necessary to maintain a roof over your head. Household. Utilities, food, fuel, car insurance and telephone service all become priorities for your organization.

In my research I found individuals believing a car payment is a priority over the mortgage or rent. Some individuals feel clothing is required before paying the utilities. When there are no parameters in place, anything goes.

Believe me, there will not be a chance of building wealth. It's not something that occurs by happenstance. You must face how you deal with money head on.

Money has never been bad or evil. The misuse of money and the passion for money has created bad and evil doings.

I have worked with people that earned the same as I did in salary. They always seemed to purchase and have the finest of everything. For years, it never really hit me that these were the same people who seemed to always be broke and borrow money for lunch from me.

They always seemed to have some kind of financial crisis going on in their lives daily. The crisis always seemed to involve the lights getting cut off or being behind on the rent or mortgage. They had fine clothes, nice cars, yet they could not pay their light bill. There was something wrong: they were "poverty-conscious."

There are three areas I believe that you must identify and then organize. Now, I will say that these areas are quite simple. They become complicated based on your belief or your desires.

Let us look at the three areas:

<u>GOD</u>	<u>HOME</u>	<u>FAMILY</u>
Tithes	Rent/ Mortgage	Entertainment
	Utilities	Cable
	Food	Child Support
	Insurance	Clothes
	Car Payment	Personal Care
	Savings	Car Repair
	Child Care	Gas
		Vacation
		Household Care

Look at how unbalanced they are.

Notice that the things required for family demand more from you. These areas can drain you of your resources.

They have a direct impact on your ability to keep financial control. It is also a support system as well because they provide comfort and convenience to the home.

God receives the least amount but gives the greatest return. It puts you in order to receive divine returns that are immeasurable. The impact is peaceful and full of serenity.

The home requires many things for maintenance. It makes the statement that your home is your castle a reality. All of these things give your organization its form.

They should become the foundation that you establish. Taking care of these things first provides a bit of security for the operation. Once you secure these areas, everything else should work off of them.

What is Your Style to Live By?

When it comes to finances, there are many different styles and groups that most people generally fall into.

In my book *Unlocking Wealth*, I identified some of the styles of how people deal with money management and their finances.

Here's a refresher:

Bargain Boomers - People that will purchase almost anything if they believe it is a good deal.

I Will Take It - Because of their inability to resist pressure by friends, family, and salespersons, they just cannot say no.

That's For Me - Giving in to the many different advertisements, they purchase items.

The Joneses - They pattern their lifestyles after others: their clothes, household items, car, and home just to name a few.

Make Me Feel Good – Retail therapy.

Oops, Let's Go Shopping - This person normally has access to money, credit cards, and a credit line without supervision or guidance.

Then you have the various groups the people fall into.

Planners – **understand** the nature of the financial goals.
Strugglers – **cannot** avoid rough financial trouble.
Deniers – **are** unwilling to accept financial direction.
Impulsive - **seek** gratification in financial matters.

If you intend to build wealth, you must have a sense of your identity, your style and your purpose. Knowing what kind of financial manager you are will help determine what changes you will make. In order to maximize your wealth-creating ability, this next section will push, I mean push you to look at your finances differently.

Creating the plan for your financial foundation (budget) is probably not the most exciting thing to do. In fact, if you have been down this road before, (setting a budget) you may feel that this is an area to skip over. I highly recommend that you read this area twice, if not more.

The principles that I will coach here are vital. This is where you realize where your money is coming from, how much is there and where it is all going. To be successful, you have to provide as much detail for your standard of living.

Ultimately, you will be able to see the difference in wealth and poverty-thinking. I want to share two stories of clients that had different experiences from creating a financial plan.

Thomas and Mary had attended many financial workshops over some years. Budgeting was one of the things that they felt strongly about.

The method that they used to set their budget required them to do a lot of gathering of financial statements, bills and other documents each month and record them.

They were tracking their spending every day each month, always having an actual total on what money they spent. Each pay period, they would sit down and determine which bill would be paid from the paycheck.

The budget that they ended up with required them to continue to pay their bills and expenses each pay period. They were comfortable with the process each month.

However, they seemed to be dissatisfied with their inability to save money and go on vacation. They were displeased with not be able to enjoy simple pleasure that did not require money.

After a few months, they were burned out from the process and just relied on paying their bills and expenses. They eventually took on another program that required them to cut off their cable services, entertainment and personal care. This was a bare bone approach to try to correct their money shortage each month.

This new program did not last long because the quality of living continued to decrease each month. This family was committed to try to find the best suitable plan that would help them. They were on a continuous search to get their finances in order.

It was not that they were over spending or taking on too much debt. No, that wasn't the problem at all. They had boxes after boxes of receipts and financial statements. There are a number of books and various programs explaining what to do with those receipts and statements.

They had probably one of the best record keeping processes that I had ever seen. Yet, they were still having problems.

Over a four-year period, they were up and down with this process. They were not adding on additional debt, their net income did not change and their spending habit was reduced. This family still could not find a way to save money or eliminate debt.

A vicious cycle had begun: a family that desired to do better was caught in the poverty mentality of not knowing what they did not know.

Now, let's look at Jake and Jada's situation. Jake and Jada had attended many financial workshops as well. They, however, worked from a different position with their finances.

Instead of gathering all of their statements every month, they simply sat down and pulled together all of their bills that were paid from the previous month.

By doing so, they were looking at the hard cost of their expenses. They determined that all of their needs were met from the previous month's expenditures and decided that they would work from there to establish their budget moving forward.

They reviewed all of their monthly utilities and created a fixed cost for all utilities. (Although the utilities varied each month, they contacted each provider and got on a budget bill payment plan.) Considering their telephone expenses, they also established a hard cost for that service as well.

On their food cost (except for eating out), they decided to make that expense a hard cost each month without going over that amount.

They reviewed what they spent on entertainment and decided that it was a bit high (due to a concert), so they decreased that amount and made it a hard cost monthly, also.

They further reviewed their personal care and household expense, and made them a fixed hard cost as well. They agreed to only make the minimum payments on all of their debts, making them a hard cost, along with car maintenance and gasoline.

What they were able to do was very simple. They reviewed all expenses paid the previous month. They were determined to make all of those that were variable expenses and turn them into hard fixed expenses based on their lifestyle.

By doing this, they created an operation cost of their home. The need to review on a month-to-month basis is not required.

They created a standard of operation on a fixed monthly number and committed themselves to it. This allowed them to have the ability to save, invest and eliminate debt.

There is no anxiety each month because they are not trying to figure out where the money is going. They effectively created the foundation to manage their money.

These two stories are a great indicator of the difference between being wealth conscious and poverty-conscious. There is an extremely huge difference between these two. We want you to recognize the difference and take the right path.

Remember that being poverty-conscious is the major reason why many people are unable to accumulate wealth. In short, you should be approaching your budget with a wealth conscious mentality.

All of your values and plans for your financial future and retirement should be on the table. If you are married, you must have that conversation with your spouse.

There was a study done in 2011. Couples Retirement Study analyzed retirement expectations and preparedness among 648 married couples (1,296 individuals).

Respondents were required to be at least 46-years-old, married and living with their respective spouses and have a minimum household income of $75,000 or at least $100,000 in investable assets.

In 2011, 196 retired couples were also represented in the study, which previously included only couples who had not yet entered retirement.

Retired couples are defined as both spouses being retired from their primary occupation, even if they continue to work in retirement.

The results show couples both approaching and living in retirement are struggling with overall communication, planning and management of their retirement finances.

With less than half of couples (41%) handling investment decisions for retirement savings jointly, the data highlights key areas for improvement on many major financial and retirement planning topics.

For example:

- Only 17% of couples are completely confident that either spouse is prepared to assume responsibility of their joint retirement finances, if necessary

- One-third (33%) of couples either don't agree, or don't know, where they plan to retire

- Nearly two-thirds (62%) of couples approaching retirement don't agree on their expected retirement ages

- Nearly half (47%) of couples approaching retirement don't agree on whether they will continue to work in retirement

- Three quarters (73%) of all couples disagree on whether or not they have completed a detailed retirement income plan

As a family/couple, you will have worked very hard to save for retirement. However, if you do not take the time, or have the comfort level and jointly discuss your plans for the future it means nothing.

You should seek the best course of action. Couples should sit down long before they retire to discuss key financial topics, such as when they plan to retire, where they want to live, whether they plan to work and what lifestyle they hope to enjoy.

Once you can agree on the vision for retirement, start the process by evaluating your essential and discretionary expenses and comparing them to anticipated sources of income, including Social Security, pensions and personal savings.

Doing so will help you assess whether they are on track to meet your retirement goals.

The study results show that wives are less involved in critical areas.

The study also found wives are often not as involved and/or are less knowledgeable about their retirement finances than husbands are – especially regarding financial confidence, engagement, awareness and approach to investing. Specifically, the data shows:

- Confidence: When asked if they feel confident that they could assume full responsibility of their household retirement finances, if needed, only 35% of wives say they are completely confident in their ability to do so vs. 72% of husbands.

- Engagement: A small percentage of wives (8%) report they are the primary retirement financial decision-maker in their household, compared to 37% of husbands. Further, fewer wives (15%) than husbands (40%) consider themselves to be the "primary contact" with their investment professional.

- Awareness: Wives/Women generally have a lower awareness of retirement income-related topics than husbands have. For instance, when asked how much money they expect their income sources to generate monthly in retirement, twice as many wives (32%) as husbands (15%) say they do not know.

- Investment Style: Wives tend to have a lower risk tolerance and invest less aggressively than husbands. For example, 21% of wives say they are most interested in preserving wealth and therefore willing to settle for lower returns vs. 16% of husbands. In addition, only 5% of wives describe themselves as investors, rather than a spender or saver, vs. 20% of husbands.

To improve joint/women retirement readiness, it was recommend that the wives/women work to:

- Understand their financial situation and savings and investment goals

- Be an active participant in all financial planning and investment decisions

- Make sure their objectives and risk tolerance are reflected in their investment strategy

- Be prepared for potential threats that could jeopardize their financial security, such as longevity, an unexpected illness or disability, inflation and/or increasing tax liabilities

- Learn as much as they can about investing and maintain an appropriate asset allocation for their age and life stage

- Know where critical documents are kept and what they would need to do if their spouse is no longer able to assist with financial decision-making

It is essential that both husbands and wives have a voice in setting and achieving financial goals and that each is comfortable asking questions and providing input on key decisions.

This is particularly important for women because they tend to outlive men and likely will need to manage the finances on their own, or work with an investment professional, later in life.

You Will... Absolutely...

You will have to pay rent or a mortgage.
You will have to pay the light bill.
You will have to pay insurance.
You will have to pay car payments.
You will have to pay the telephone bill.
You will have to pay credit card bills.
You will pay for maintenance.
You will pay for car repair.
You will have to buy groceries.
You will have to buy clothes.
You will have to buy household supplies.

You absolutely have to create a budget.
You absolutely have to manage money.
You absolutely have to control spending.
You absolutely have to save money.
You absolutely have to invest money.
You absolutely have to eliminate debt.
You absolutely have to accumulate wealth.
You absolutely have to create a retirement plan.

What you should have learned is this chapter:

1. Budgeting puts you on the road to being wealth-conscious, yet it may seem that you are more poverty-conscious because of the stance you have to take.

2. By establishing financial control in your home, your family's organization is established. Your primary role in this organization is to create the control in which you will operate.

3. To be successful, you have to understand every detail to establish your standard of living.
4. All of your values and plans for your financial future and retirement should be on the table.
5. It's essential that both husbands and wives have a voice in setting and achieving financial goals.

Chapter 3

Creating a Budget To Live By

Budget! Budget! Budget!

Before I guide you into setting up the last financial foundation, you should ever need, I want to recapture some of the things I talked about with a different angle to ensure that you see this process in a different way.

First, I did say your last financial foundation. You are about to build and create wealth for your future and the future of your children's children. A foundation that is established correctly will allow you to grow and expand.

Every household will bring a unique situation. There are no cookie cutter ways to put your financial numbers in order.

However, when you do it correctly (in a way that is suited for your family), it will allow you to be in a better position that will help define your success.

There are no rules to guarantee success, there are things that drive us and put us on the right track. There will be some rules of thumb that can help you progress.

So, I ask you, "Why do you have to create a budget? Isn't this book about wealth accumulation?"

This book is about wealth accumulation. However, my question, "Why do you have to create a budget?" is vital for you to answer for yourself.

From what I have experienced on the radio and during one on one consulting, I have found that most people start to get help or start looking to change their money habits when they want something.

You want to try to eliminate credit card debt.
You want to save for a new car, or to buy your first house.
You want to go on vacation.
You want to pay for college tuition.

I know everyone has unique financial situations that are bigger than setting goals right now. Regardless of your approach, there is a certain way that you want to live. That alone should generate financial goals.

Whatever your goals are, they are your goals and nobody else's. It's not appropriate to question anybody else's goals or have yours questioned by anybody else, **except for me right now.**

Because you have financial goals, I want you to elevate your thinking. This is the time for you to really evaluate your own mentality and determine where you are.

That is the one thing that I cannot do or give you. I will give you reasons to help you move forward with a wealth consciousness rather than the poverty-consciousness mentality.

Here are some reasons why you should budget:

Set and prioritize financial goals	Figure out how to get out of debt
Be a smarter consumer	Curb impulse purchases
Get a grip on your spending	Build a cash fund
Pay your bills on time	Start a savings program
Find ways to cut costs	Learn to live within your means
Live on less money so you can work less	Distinguish between wants and needs
Meet your family's changing financial needs	Reduce stress associated with saving for big expenses
Stop making ends meet with a credit card	Sleep at night without worrying about your bills
Stop living from paycheck to paycheck	

These are the normal things that we hear about every day, and, for the most part, it has no impact on getting you to change.

These are reasons—good reasons—to put together a budget. But, you know this already.

So, why hasn't this method worked in the past? Just about every financial expert that I come across uses these reasons to motivate people to start budgeting. It has not worked.

Let me try to be clear here. Each of those reasons should be a part of your overall deliberation. In fact, these reasons are like the inner workings of the shift from poverty-consciousness to wealth-consciousness.

I understood and considered that most financial educators use rules and guidelines to create a budget. Like the reason that I just discussed, these rules and guidelines are like the inner workings of the shift from poverty-consciousness to wealth-consciousness.

Rules and Guidelines to Create a Budget:

Assess your monthly expenses	Gather every financial statement you can
Total your earnings	Record all of your sources of income
Subtract expenses from earnings	Create a list of monthly expenses
Rework your budget	Break expenses into 2 categories: fixed and variable
Build in money for debt reduction	Make adjustments to expenses
Build in your savings and investments	Total your monthly income and monthly expenses
Put your budget to work	Review your budget monthly
Assess your budget	Assess and assess again

Just like the reasons why you should budget, these are normal things that we hear about every day and for the most part, it has no impact on getting you to change. These are rules—good rules—to put together a budget and you know this already.

So, why haven't these reasons, rules and guidelines worked? Many say it is because of FEAR (False Evidence Appearing Real): fear of having constraint in place, not being able to dine out, not being able buy clothes or to enjoy life.

When the benefits of creating a budget are explained and made clear, people have a tendency to still panic and give up.

Knowing that having a budget will provide you with the freedom and flexibility of surviving a layoff, buying something you want guilt-free, remodeling the kitchen, buying a new iPhone or taking a vacation.

If you want to dine out, pay for your children's education, pay down your debts or buy a home or car, you will need a budget.

The benefits are compromised because of the fear of the word BUDGET. This word really seems to be a mountain to climb for many people. Learning to conquer this fear is the most important benefit in this learning process.

The bottom line is you cannot create financial freedom and accumulate wealth without overcoming the way you approach budgeting.

Once you have created a budget, it often sounds and looks good on paper. For most people, it is hard to execute and maintain.

If you are fearful and tired of failing to create a budget for you or your family, the problem might be that you simply have not changed your mindset.

Your mindset towards budgeting is an important part of creating a healthy financial lifestyle as you grow older. The sooner you realize the difference between wealth conscious and poverty-conscious the more successful you will be with money for the rest of your life.

Let's look at something for a moment. Businesses of all sizes, both public and private, need budgets to meet their financial goals. Those who try to handle financial goals without it often are the first to fail.

If you know how to drive a car, it is very likely that you can drive a van, a truck or a bus. Driving becomes a skill that you learn. With driving, there are things required that you learn about the vehicle (brakes, turn signals, warning lights and so on). Your personal budget is very similar in that it helps you to reach specific financial goals.

Most people prefer to stay in a comfort zone when it comes to dealing with money. I cannot understand why a person would rather cash their paycheck at a check cashing location and not use a bank.

Nor can I understand why someone would prefer to borrow money in advance of receiving his or her paycheck. All of these things are done because of fear.

The fear of not making ends meet each month, not even considering the outcome. A good example of that is a payday loan.

A person with an income of $1,200 a month without a budget sees a need for an additional $200 to meet monthly expenses. So they borrow $200 and will need to repay $250 in thirty days.

When that due date approaches, they pay the $250 out of the $1,200 that reduces the income to $950, which now requires them to have a greater need.

Sometimes, they will just only pay the $50 and keep the process going and still create a need to borrow more money. The fear of setting a budget will give you a blurred picture.

Any type of fear that serves as a boundary that prohibits individuals from moving forward is the same type of fear that can hinder a person from successfully accumulating wealth.

They are afraid that there will be too many life changes, so they refuse to let go. Fear is no more than what I call **personal deceit**. This is where you deceive yourself into believing that you will fail.

Finally, I am going to share an email that a client sent as I was writing this chapter of the book. Almost a year has passed since this client paid and signed up for a personal financial makeover.

These are her exact words: *I paid for this many months ago. I remember hearing you talk once before and you said that you had a client and it took her some months to complete the budget and send it back and you didn't understand why;*

Well I can tell you why: the same thing happened to me. FEAR overtakes you and all kinds of things go thru your head. I did have something to lose by not doing this sooner and that FEAR just kept me stuck.

Fear of not doing something right and being a failure in front of my children and husband because they don't believe in this -- they are sort of waiting to see what happens with me then they will listen more attentively.

Fear of messing up and not following your directions closely. Just plain ole fear --

Well, I finally had to get over myself because I have been listening to you for the longest and I said to myself -- get up off your AZZ and let the fear go there and you do what he says.

As you can see, fear is real and can lock you down like nothing I have ever seen. I am not going to give FEAR (False Evidence Appearing Real) any more attention in this book. Budgets are used for many reasons and by many people.

Remember, we are working towards Wealth Increasing Now. Yes, living within your means is an important step toward your long-term financial stability, and knowing how to make a personal budget is critical.

My goal for your budget is to help you identify how you will spend your money, set your financial goals and track your spending to ensure that you achieve them.

Creating your personal budget will take some effort, but once you create the wealth conscious habits, you're on your way to financial security and accumulating wealth.

The worst thing that you can do is start your budget right after you have had a major crisis in your life. I know some of my colleagues would say that is the right time to budget. A sound mind and focus is going to be required for you to be successful with creating a budget.

The actual strength and vision that is necessary will require you to have your finances on a steady pace. I have recommended to clients to wait two to three months after going through a crisis before starting a budget.

Life happens, and when you set goals and purpose in your life for the future, something seems to always happen. I had a client that recently created their financial road map (budget). It's complete with short, medium and long-term goals.

This budget was really fully thought out. She had savings, debt reduction, investments and a just in case savings plan incorporated.

She had made plans for any unforeseen events like the car breaking down or the roof-needing repair. What she did not plan for was that her dog would die. Sadly, her dog broke away from her chasing a cat and was struck by a car.

This type of tragedy is something you cannot plan. In addition, what does this have to do with money? If her budget was complete with consideration of things popping up, where is the problem? The problem is her mental capacity; she is now depressed, finding it hard to focus.

She just lost a beloved member of her family. Things like this can and will happen. So, it is very important to delay the start date if you have to, only for a short period of time. Always remember that delay is not denial.

I have heard that it is required that you should review your budget for several months, but you must commit to it. The reason behind this statement is that you are not going to stay on track.

Understand that your plan is going to create some anxiety for you, due to the changes you will now have to make. It is going to discourage you from wanting to continue. I completely disagree with that approach.

This is another view of that poverty mentality that I have been talking about. If it is not clear to you now, by the time, you complete this chapter, you will understand.

I want to have some fun with you. I am going to challenge you with a brief test. This test is relying on you to be quick, honest and truthful.

Below are three quick questions that I want you to answer. In order to do this correctly and fairly, you must use the first answer that pops into your mind.

1. The iPad is a line of tablet computers designed and marketed by:
a. Banana Joe
b. Apple Inc.
c. Burger King

2. What is an app:
a. Software
b. Fruit
c. Vegetable

3. The first iPad was released in:
a. November 1999
b. December 2000
c. April 2010

Now, how easy was that? Consider your pattern of thinking.

Was it quick or slow? That is really what I was getting at. I know I made it easier for you by using some crazy answers. I really want you to see how simple it is to know what is realistic.

Okay, you think I just lost it here. I did briefly lose my focus and that happens sometimes. However, my journey was very short and I am getting back to my wealth mentality to finish this book. Oops!

Your Net Income Is The Key

As we move closer to creating your budget, we must take a look at the primary element that makes all of your efforts to accumulate wealth happen. Exactly what is considered as your net income?

First, let's just look at income—there is gross income. It is all the money that you earn, usually generated as compensation in the form of a paycheck.

Gross incomes can come from many sources and takes many forms, both for services rendered and goods sold. It may be rent from property, sales and sales commissions or professional retainer fees.

Salary	Royalties
Rents	Dividends
Pensions	Annuities
Alimony	Interest
Any income from life insurance	Any income related to a decedent

41

Income from endowment contracts	Separate maintenance payments
The gross profit that has been derived from business	Income from any interest in an estate or maybe a trust
Compensation for any services which includes fees, commissions or fringe benefits	The gains derived from any dealings in property

When you get your salary on your pay stub, you will notice that the word gross income is mentioned. It is the total amount that you make before all the taxes have been deducted.

In fact, you can also say that gross income is the sum total of all the income that a person earns. The sources of the income are not that important.

For many, net income is referred to as take home pay or the amount of money earned after all payroll withholdings such as state and federal income taxes, Social Security taxes, and pretax benefits like health insurance premiums.

If you are enrolled in a flexible spending account to pay for medical costs, the amount withheld from each check is also on a pre-tax basis. If you are enrolled in a company sponsored pension or 401k, these deductions are taken from your pay as well.

Payroll taxes must be withheld from your paycheck. This is required by law. Your employers must hand these withholdings over to various tax agencies.

Net income is gross income less deductions. Payroll tax deductions include the following:

Payroll Tax Deductions	Payroll Deductions
Social Security tax withholding	Life insurance premiums
State income tax withholding	Employee stock purchase plans
Federal income tax withholding	Health insurance premiums (medical, dental and eye care)
Medicare tax withholding	Retirement plan contributions (such as a 401k plan)
Various tax withholdings (city, county, or school district taxes, state disability or unemployment insurance)	Meals, uniforms, union dues and other job-related expenses

Voluntary deductions can be paid with pre-tax dollars or after-tax dollars, depending on the type of benefit being paid for.

I still encounter people who do not have a clue of their earnings. Let me point this out right here and now. Not knowing what your gross and net income is shows your disconnect with your own money.

Before you move forward from here, please review your check stub, payroll statement and any other document that shows you your income.

It is true that income can take various forms: some are simple while others are complicated; some are regular, others are not; a few are one-time windfalls, while still others come in small streams. It differs with every individual so there are different methods of computing them.

But at the end of the day, you must know what your total net income is. Having a wealth mentality requires you to know your money.

Listen, I can go down the list of things that you have complete detail of: mobile apps, video games, iPhone, iPads, iPods, Facebook, Twitter and many other devices and apps.

Unfortunately, none of these can secure or protect your financial future. And the fact that you can explain them clearly to others shows that you have a relationship with them.

But you do not know your total net income? **Now you understand my crazy questions a few pages back!**

It should be simple for you to know your net income. It's the money that comes into your personal household, which is usually generated as pay in the form of a paycheck for work you have done.

There are many different sources of this net income that includes the things that we talked about. We identified the forms of income as passive income, which is generated when you rent out rooms, homes or apartments, or you earn capital gains, interest or dividends on investments or interest bearing accounts like savings accounts or some checking accounts.

There is income that comes from selling goods or services by doing a side job, getting paid for consulting services or selling products. There is also income from royalties, which are gained from agreements made related to copyrights, patents, or gas, mineral or petroleum properties.

Always refer to your net income as your take home pay if it is easier for you. Keep in mind that the amount of money you earned will have payroll withholding as we discussed such as state and federal income taxes, Social Security taxes, and pretax benefits like health insurance premiums.

Sometimes, there may be loans (car, 401k loan) that are deducted from your check as well. Your net Income is income less any/all of those deductions.

Be sure not to confuse your gross pay (money earned before taxes or deductions) with your net income (take home pay after taxes and deductions.)

Carefully read your check stub, which includes itemization of gross pay and the taxes and pre-tax deductions. Even if you have direct deposit, you should get a record of each check with these details.

Be sure that you pay attention to the "Net Pay", remember this number as if it was your social security number or birthday. Everything you do financially should start from realizing the number.

Period:	7/20/2012	Employee Name	Check Number	10008103
Tax Status	1	Federal Allowance	1	
Hourly Rate	Salary	Overtime Rate	$0.00	
Social Sec. Tax	$114.85	Federal Tax	$265.02	
Medicare Tax	$26.43	State Tax	$23.70	
Insurance	$20.00		$0.00	
Total Taxes Deductions	$450.00		$0.00	
Year To Date		Hours Worked	80	
Federal Tax	$2,836.15	Sick Hours	0	
Social Security Tax	$1,310.02	Vacation Hours	0	
State Tax	$2,158.24	Overtime	0	
		Gross Pay	**$1,823.00**	
		Total Deductions	$440.20	
		Net Pay	**$1,382.80**	

A Motivational Quote

Live your dream now. What will your life be like when you have achieved your most deeply held dreams? Let's take a look at how you can start living your dreams this very day.

Do you have a dream, a vision of the life you wish to live? How specific is that dream? How clear is that vision? How do you intend to reach it? What obstacles stand in your way? To reach that dream you have to see yourself reaching it.

46

See yourself beyond your present circumstances. See that you will change those circumstances. See yourself beyond the challenges and you will overcome those challenges. You have GREATNESS within you!!

- Les Brown is a dynamic personality and highly-sought-after renowned motivational speaker.

What you should have learned in this chapter:

1. A foundation that is established correctly will allow you to grow and expand.
2. When you establish a foundation in a manner that is correctly suited for your family, it will allow you to be in a better position that will help define success.
3. There are no rules to guarantee success.
4. Regardless of your approach, there is a certain way that you want to live. That alone should generate financial goals.
5. Whatever your goals are, they are your goals and nobody else's.
6. There are specific reasons why you should budget.
7. There are rules and guidelines in creating a budget.
8. Having a budget will provide you with the freedom and flexibility of surviving a layoff.
9. You cannot create financial freedom and accumulate wealth without overcoming the way you approach budgeting.
10. The sooner you realize the difference between wealth-consciousness and poverty-consciousness, the more successful you will be with money the rest of your life.

11. Fear serves as a boundary that prohibits individuals from moving forward. It can hinder a person from successfully accumulating wealth.
12. Your net income is the key.
13. Not knowing what your gross and net income is shows your disconnect with your own money.
14. Having a wealth mentality requires you to know your money.

Chapter 4

Meet the Blair Family

Not establishing and knowing your net income is a sure sign that you will fail. To help you move forward, I am sharing a story of one of the best results of all of my coaching. I will break it down in different parts to ensure that I am clear.

I want to share the story of Tom and Sally Blair. They were heavily loaded down with over $49,900 of unsecure debt.
They were able to change their mentality from poverty-minded to wealth-consciousness. They were able to eliminate this debt and build $255,000 in wealth in 7½ years.

Sally Blair took in account all of the income that she had coming in each month. These incomes were consistent each month, so it was simple to get a total. After taking in account the income of her spouse as well, their total net income was $5,000 a month.

They were very confused at first because they were living paycheck to paycheck. At the end of each month, there was less than $200 remaining. There was no budget, no order with their finances and no real financial goals set.

In fact, they really did not know how much money was coming into the house. They knew that they got paid very well, and each week when one of them got paid, they simply wrote checks and sent them off.

Most people handle money this way. On payday, they check to see if the direct deposit made it to the bank. They check the balance and then determine what will be paid. If there is something going on that week (concerts, sporting event or school event), it means something may not be paid.

Therefore, my first goal was to challenge them about what they were really doing and what they wanted. I found out, like most people, they did have financial goals. But they were all in their heads and much different from each other.

They wanted to have an education fund for their child, they wanted to have money to go on a vacation and they did not want to rely on Social Security to survive in retirement.

Chances are your household operates like the Blairs. You both have financial goals that are similar but these goals are stuck in your head. But this is good to realize because it makes your transition easier than someone who does not have any goals at all.

Now that she has a clear knowledge of the household income and the exact penny that comes in each month the tough part begins.

This is where I recommend that you put the book down and clear your head for a few minutes. As you do so, think of who you are, what you do every day, then every month. Get to know you.

The Blair Story

What I asked the Blairs to do was to tell me a story about their life. Of course, they looked at me a little funny, so I led them into their story.

Tell me! What does your family do or like to do each month for fun?

We occasionally like to go out for dinner or eat out.
We enjoy going to the movies.
(Laughing). The family likes to ice skate around the holidays.
Son plays school sports.

Tell me! What do you do for personal care?

Mrs. Blair: I would like to get my hair done more often.
Mr. Blair: Just the basic personal hygiene.

Tell me! How often do you buy clothes?

About twice a year, mostly around school and Christmas time.

Tell me! Do you belong to any type of club where there is a fee?

The kids are in chess and tennis clubs.

So, I asked them to think more about the four questions and see if they left anything out. They determined that was it for the most part.

Now, I want you to answer the very same questions. This is your time (Me Time) to sit down and think about your family story. What you do or would like to do? Be very realistic, just as the Blair family was. If you need to stop here and take a moment to answer these questions, I highly recommend it.

The very next thing we talked about in the family story was a little more personal.

Tell me! Your car: is it new or used and do you have a payment on it?

Our car is a few years old. We have about two more years of payments. We have a second car that is paid for.

Tell me! Do you have any car maintenance expenses?

No, just regular oil changes. We may need to buy some tires soon.

Tell me! Do you have many miles to drive during the week?

Oh yes, back and forth to school and work. Sometimes, we can get away with only one car because I work from home.

Tell me! How many cell phones do you have?

We have a package deal that includes our two cell phones and a land line phone as well as cable.

All of this in one package?

Yes, somewhat. We paid a certain amount for all three services separately and get a great discount on all of them.

Tell me! How often do you go to the grocery store each month?

Right now that is crazy. We go every week and sometimes twice in a week.

Why is that?

Because we forget something or run out of some things, like milk and stuff.

Tell me! Do you have any type of insurance that you are paying directly?

Yes, we pay car insurance each month and we have some life insurance.

Tell me! Are there any other children outside of the marriage that you are responsible for or that someone else is responsible to you?

NO, there'd better not be. (Laughing.)

Then we took a break and they began to ask me why I was asking all of those questions. I told them that I was trying to know the family. At this point, I truly hope that you are writing down your answers to the questions.

Think about something here. As we were talking, they realized that often times there are day-to-day things that just come up. They have to make a decision To Do Something.

That got me to thinking about how different each family really is. Your family has things that you do personally and together. Those things seem to be the things that make you who you are.

Like the Blair family, you like to go out for dinner or eat out, you like going to the movies, you like family trips for the holidays and your children may play school sports.

You care about getting your hair done and your basic personal hygiene as well as buying clothes for your family, having your kids in clubs or private schools, taking a family vacation, maintaining your car, enjoying your cell phones, cable and feeding your family.

Being able to provide the insurance coverage that your family needs is no different from any other family. This is what I want to express to you the most. There are some absolutes in life that each of us must face. These absolutes are often similar in nature, but different by our culture and mentality.

Listen, I realize with the rising costs of food, gas and insurance, so many people are spending more time focusing on how to make ends meet. Facing a crawling economy with the possibility of layoffs looming, it's hard to concentrate on trying to have financial accomplishment.

Almost at a point of giving up or ignoring financial obligations to your family is not an option. Although you may feel overwhelmed and not able to make it, there always seems to be food to eat and a roof over your head.

The struggling and fighting to maintain might not bring financial security faster. Letting go of the fear of deprivation and poverty will be extremely liberating. This is why I trust you answered each of those questions honestly.

Now, let's get back to the Blair family. They have a lot of other stuff to reveal to us. I had to dig a little deeper into their family. They were not really feeling me at this point. Mr. Blair asked if we were going to talk about their finances at all. I replied.

Tell me! Are you a family of faith? If so, do you pay tithes and offerings?

Mrs. Blair: Yes, we are and yes, we do.

Tell me! Are you buying your home? Is that correct?

Yes, we are. However, we are thinking about walking away.

Walking away?

Yes, we see homes all around us going into foreclosure or being abandoned.

Tell me! What does that have to do with you?

The property value has dropped for the last few years.

Tell me! Are you able to keep your lights and utilities paid?

Yes, we have been able to manage.

Tell me! Do you have any credit cards?

Yes, five of them.

At this point, Mr. Blair was taking on the protector role. "Mr. Wilson, you come highly recommended and we believe that you can help us. I do not know why you haven't asked about our finances."

I said to him, "I understand that, Sir. I have not asked to see the numbers yet. We will get there. I promise."

Therefore, without much waiting, I went there. **Tell me about these five credit cards that you have.**

Mr. Blair, with a smile, begins to say that the credit cards are all high interest rate cards. He then went on to give me all the reasons why each of them was at their credit limit.

Tell me! Are you paying them each month?

Oh, yes…

Tell me! Are you making the minimum payments on them all?

Oh, no. We are paying more depending on the balance.

May I ask why?

We want to get them paid off before we get too old.

Tell me! What is the total of your credit card debt?

Let me see. It is $49,800

Tell me! What is the lowest interest rate on one of your cards?

16% and the highest is 22%.

Tell me! What do you expect from all of this?

We want to get on a path to have financial security. We are SO fed up living paycheck to paycheck. We want to send our children to college, pay off our home and save money for retirement.

Are you saving money now?

We do, but we always seem to go into it for something every month.

At this point, they became very emotional. We took a break. If you are really reading this and have answered all of the questions yourself, you should be emotional as well.

As I share their answers to my questions, I hope that I am getting you to look at your family and your financial situation in a different way. I told you that this is about a wealth mentality versus a poverty mentality. If I could get you to accept that you are struggling, it will NOT be hard for you to see the better side of things.

The questions below are the very same questions that the Blair family had to answer. If you did not take the time to answer the questions honestly for your household, here is your second chance. This is a critical part for you.

What does your family do or like to do each month for fun?
What do you do for personal care?
How often do you buy clothes?
Do you belong to any type of club where there is a fee?
Your car: is it new or used, do you have a payment on it?
Do you have any car maintenance expenses?
Do you have many miles to drive during the week?
How many cell phones do you have?
How often do you go to the grocery store each month? Why is that?
Do you have any type of insurance that you are paying directly?
Are there any other children outside of the marriage that you are responsible for or that someone else is responsible to you?

Are you a family of faith? If so, do you pay tithes and offerings?
Are you buying your home?
Are you able to keep your lights and utilities paid regularly?
Do you have any credit cards?
Are you paying them each month?
Are you making the minimum payments on them all? May I ask why?
What is the total of your credit card debt?
What is the lowest interest rate on one of your cards?
Are you saving money now?

Do you remember how we separated the three areas for your home in Chapter 2? The three areas provide comfort and security for your family.

What I was doing with the Blair family was identifying their home foundation (budget). When you are setting up your foundation, it will take a little work.

Instead of tracking what you spend, you begin with how you live. How you live becomes the blueprint of the foundation (budget). Each week, you may eat out for lunch and it costs you $15 a week to do so. Once a month, you may enjoy going to the movies with the family; that may cost $50 along with popcorn and sodas. That establishes an entertainment cost of $110 a month.

This is what I was getting the Blair family to see. I know that most of my colleagues would tell you to cut back, cut things off. I want you to preserve everything that makes you who you are. How dare someone tell you to cut back as a first option?

I do believe that at some point cutting back may be a necessary thing to do. Here is the challenge: How do you secure your family without converting to that beans and rice strategy? That is what this process is all about.

So how did we do this?

You remember that in Chapter 2 I talked about these three areas below as the center of creating a budget. These things represent who you are. When the core of your financial foundation is not in place, nothing else matters.

Look at them again, think of the questions that I asked. Are you getting the bigger picture?

GOD	HOME	FAMILY
Tithes	Rent/Mortgage	Entertainment
	Utilities	Cable
	Child Support	Food
	Insurance	Clothes
	Car Payment	Personal Care
	Savings	Car Repair
	Child Care	Gas
		Vacation
		Household Care

These three areas must be secured at all times. This is the family vanguard (standard of living). You will have the ability to increase it and/or move costs around, but you should never decrease it. That changes your family's lifestyle. This is your foundational position that allows everything else to happen.

After The Break – The Results

Mr. Blair wanted to get to the results. His patience had grown very thin by this point. Most of us want results right away, never considering fully the outcome of the decision.

This is where I need you to experience the transitions from a poverty mindset to a wealth mentality. You will feel the need to get quick results. There is nothing wrong with that as long as the foundation is set and your goals are clear.

So we began to set numbers, real numbers to their answers to the questions that I had previously asked. I asked them to tell me a story about the family and their life/lifestyle. This is how I communicated back to them: So, you stated that you occasionally go out for dinner, enjoy going to the movies, ice skating, and your son plays school sports.

Eating out: $75; Ice skating: $35; the movies: $30.
Getting your hair done and basic personal hygiene: Personal care: $75; Seasonal clothing: $75.
The kids' club fees (chess & tennis): $300 a year.
Your car payment is $350 a month. Your maintenance is $25 a month.
Gas for your car is $80. Your cable is $45, your cell phone is $75. Your food cost is $250.
Your car insurance is $100 a month and life insurance is $38 a month. You pay tithes and offerings: $200.
You are buying your home: $785.
Your light bill is $50, your gas is $50, your water and sewer is $25.

Your balances on your credit card are:

Credit Card 1: $14,500.00
Credit Card 2: $11,000.00
Credit Card 3: $5,300.00
Credit Card 4: $11,000.00
Credit Card 5: $8,000.00

Total debt is $49,800. You are saving $175 every month. This is how all of the numbers looked as they provided them to me. Of course, I had to make some changes.

The Blair Family Household Expenses

Tithes	$200.00	Life Ins.	$38.00
Mortgage	$785.00	Auto Ins.	$100.00
Savings	$175.00	Personal Care	$75.00
Water	$10.00	Entertainment	$140.00
Sewer	$10.00	Gasoline	$80.00
Gas	$50.00	Car Repair	$25.00
Lights	$50.00	Clothes	$75.00
Cable	$45.00	Club Fees	$25.00
Telephone	$75.00	Household	$50.00
Food	$250.00	Car Payment	$350.00

House Expenses $2,608.00

These are the results of the answers to my questions. As you can see, I am only showing the three areas that I believe are the most important aspect of having a financial foundation.

However, as I review the critical numbers (the numbers that make them who they are), they are numbers that I believe are acceptable for this family.

If there were expenses that seem to be outrageous, then we would consider making some changes. Mr. Blair was thrilled to hear that this area was okay.

Let's forget about the debt for right now. This home foundation has a surplus of $150, considering debt payments. It does not allow you many different options for goal setting.

This surplus should provide you the ability to increase your tithes, to increase your savings, and the ability to look at other areas to invest. Also, there is little room to increase your entertainment and your personal care. All of this is possible to see only because the household is organized.

That was not hard at all. What we did was establish a standard to live by. Most people have a fake standard of living anyway. It fakes you out every other month to the point that you really cannot understand or see where your money is going. This is about creating the foundation and having a wealth mentality. This is a moment that you can claim and begin to see a road to prosperity.

It all begins with how you manage what you currently have. Your desire for more comes when you are not taking care of what you have. It really puts you in that, "I'm ready to be deceived mode." That poverty mentality has held you back for too long.

As the manager of your home, you are able to establish a vision that allows you to view the process without risk. Many of my colleagues believe that you cannot build wealth without risk. Let me say it another way. You cannot have prosperity without risk. Do not believe the hype.

I have taught thousands of people how to use this foundational approach (budget). Many have tried just about everything and said, "Why not?" Once they learned how simple it was to set-up and then manage their financial foundation, they realized how misguided they were from all of the other methods they had tried.

This will work with any family. There may always be a need to make adjustments. No adjustment should be that dramatic, and create such discomfort in the family. It is not money that causes marriages to suffer or end in divorce.

Money is not the root of all evil. The passion to chase after and to love money creates evil. Likewise, with marriages, it is not knowing how to deal with money that separates families.

Well, we must talk about another area; the area I believe intimidates most people. This is like a cancer to your finances.

Once you create it, it seems to continue to grow and eat away at your life's savings. So, let's take a look at eliminating debt by cutting it out, chunks at a time. Using the financial foundation approach (budget), we will add in the Blair family's debt totals.

So, why is this family living paycheck to paycheck each month? Where are the challenges that seem to create a shortage each month?

Let's go back to the answers that they provided in their story,. When I asked them about their credit card debt, Mr. Blair stated that they are paying more than the minimum payment on the credit cards.

His reasoning is simply this, he has heard if you are making only the minimum payment you will never get out of debt. That is the type of direction and guidance that most of all the financial coaches and experts I know provide.

I do not subscribe to that type of teaching. I do accept the fact the making minimum payments only without a strategy can and will result in an endless attempt to get out of debt.

I teach strategy first. Making the minimum payment with a strategic plan of action allows you the freedom to eliminate debt and build wealth.

As you see with the Blair's numbers, the reason that they do not have a more solid financial foundation is due to following incomplete advice. Let us look at their debts and payments.

The Blair Family's Debt

Debts	Current Payments	Balances
Credit Card 1	$580.00	$14,500.00
Credit Card 2	$520.00	$11,000.00
Credit Card 3	$367.00	$5,300.00
Credit Card 4	$450.00	$11,000.00
Credit Card 5	$325.00	$8,000.00
	$2,242.00	**$49,800.00**

This can be intimidating to any household.

The problem that the Blair family has is simple. They have made a commitment to travel the wrong road. We all have made a wrong choice in life at some point.

64

The Blairs knew that something needed to be done. Speaking to them about this, they share some interesting news. In fact, they have attended some classes and became a member of the debt free club.

This club had fees of $49 a month and they met twice a month to discuss a payback plan. The Blairs were not able to explain what the plan was supposed to do for them. They set up pay back bags each month to send to each credit card.

This action was a part of their total overall frustration, and I understood why. The only people that benefited from that club were the organizers.

Once you determine that you want financial freedom, you must set goals that are relative to your family. There is a lot of information out there; most of it sounds the same.

As I mentioned in earlier chapters, knowing the difference between a poverty mentality and a wealth mentality becomes the first step to financial freedom.

Every decision that you make has a cost associated with it. This cost will either bring you closer to your financial goals or move you farther away. I know that it has been difficult. I know that you have tried and have done the best that you know how.

Now, step back. Make a commitment to make wealth-consciousness decisions in every action of your life. Determine the financial impact of all decisions made. Focus on providing a way of life for you and your family first.

This is what I want your foundation to do for you. Secure the needs of your household and maintain a standard of living that suits you, not the Joneses. Honor your faith, enjoy activities with your family, and enjoy the comfort of your home.

Next, protect that way of life for your household. Why do we do things the way that we do them? Most of the time, it comes down to our emotions and fear.

Our emotions can influence financial decisions in surprisingly predictable ways. We tend to be overconfident in our own knowledge and decisions. We extrapolate recent trends while dismissing the past, and we refuse to accept losses gracefully by hanging on to them far too long, and so on. Do not allow what I just said to negatively affect you. Even experienced investors and savers are not immune.

Frequently, we make what we firmly believe to be rational decisions, but those decisions are primarily based on the input of our own emotions, not ideas, data or analysis. Sometimes the emotional displays of people close to us affect our decision-making.

There was a study I read regarding the areas of the brain responsible for our emotional states, and how it powerfully influences how we think about risks and rewards.

It found that subjects unknowingly made less risky investment decisions after viewing a picture associated with negative affects versus those viewing neutral pictures. When we see our financial life in a neutral position, we are okay taking risks.

Engaging our consciousness gives rise to the ability to survey the range of possibilities and optimize our decision-making. The advantages of reasoning, deliberation and planning are remarkable. We simply cannot run our lives, our portfolios, or our businesses without deliberate thinking.

To understand why, consider that conscious thinking requires emotions, feelings and intuition. Unconsciously, our emotions allow us to identify ideas and thoughts as good, bad or indifferent.

People with brain damage in the areas of the brain that process emotion are incapable of making rational decisions, even though the parts of the brain responsible for reasoning are fully intact.

Moreover, an unemotional bad decision provides us no lift; no incentive to improve our decision making in the future. There is no doubt that emotions improve the quality of our decisions.

As you move towards protecting your family financially, consider the impact of your decision. Set goals as we did here with the Blairs.

If you recall, Mr. Blair became emotional after I asked him about his credit card debt and savings. He explained that he was at his limit living paycheck to paycheck. What you are about to see is why they were living paycheck to paycheck.

As you can see below, with the current payments made to reduce their debt, the total of debt payments is $2,242 a month.

When you add that to the household expenses total of $2,608, they only had $150 remaining from their $5,000 net income each month.

Debts	Current Payments	Balances
Credit Card 1	$580.00	$14,500.00
Credit Card 2	$520.00	$11,000.00
Credit Card 3	$367.00	$5,300.00
Credit Card 4	$450.00	$11,000.00
Credit Card 5	$325.00	$8,000.00
Totals	**$2,242.00**	**$49,800.00**

Remember their purpose is to get out of debt in a shorter and more reasonable period. This type of financial coaching dominates the internet and airwaves. So, I get it. I understand why so many people approach their financial life with this "get out of debt" mentality.

One of my personal mentors once told me that I had to decide what type of financial coach I wanted to be. I told him that I wanted to be one that coaches financial freedom and wealth building or getting out of debt and being debt free.

He then said, "I am an homeless man. I am debt free and I have no assets."

That statement and that statement alone drove me to take action. It made me redefine my own mission. It demanded me to create vision with purpose as a financial coach.

My purpose here is clear. It is to teach financial freedom and wealth building in a way that will influence your family for generations to come.

Action Influence

Action Influence is a new paradigm shift that I have discovered in my research for writing this book. There must be a shift in rediscovering your core financial desires. Understanding that the rules of wealth are steadfast requires a complete shifting of your commitment to create wealth.

Each generation cycle is faced with this paradigm shift. Those who recognize the shift adjust and focus on creating wealth for the next generation. They see that action is required if they are to become successful. So again, what is **Action Influence?**

Action Influence is simply taking the definition of paradigm and applying its meaning to influence your financial decision.

(**Paradigm** - A set of assumptions, concepts, values and practices that constitutes a way of viewing reality for the community that shares them, especially in an intellectual discipline.)

You must create a **set of assumptions** for your financial life. These assumptions, as a result, become the financial goals that you will set.

You must create **concepts** to implement and put your assumptions to work. These concepts are the planning practices to save, invest and eliminate debt.

You must establish your personal **values** as it relates to your assumptions and your concepts.

69

These values allow you to place in order the necessary goals and methods for accomplishing them once they are prioritized.

By taking these actions, your daily **practice** will now **constitute** a way of life and how you review the **reality** of your financial goals. It will require discipline.

In order for **Action Influence** to become a paradigm shift for you, the mindset has to change. Most people operate under a paradigm of some kind, either by decision or by default. It is referred to as learned behavior. Any one paradigm may not necessarily be fair or right; it is measured by the required traits of its definition.

Action Influence paradigm shift is creating a framework containing all of the commonly accepted views about finance, a structure of what direction you should take and how it should be performed.

It is also about knowing the difference between poverty and wealth, having a fundamental change in your individual views and that of society. You will need a committed practice that constitutes new discipline at a certain point in time.

The very **Action** that you take in organizing your financial life as I am describing in this book, over time, will branch out into your behavior and the power and **Influence** to grow your wealth.

So many things affect your behavior and play a major role in how you act at different times and in different places. Many of our lack of sound money skills affect our ability to manage money. Our spending behavior is guided by the influence of things that we are exposed to. That "live for to-day" approach or that "I deserved this" attitude is often times influenced by social experiences. As a result, these experiences alter and shape our actions.

I want you to learn that your financial position, whether it is tragic or not, can control the outlook of your financial life in just a few decisive actions.

Action Influence can give you a unique approach to achieving your financial goals. When you embrace the challenges faced by your household finances and apply goal-oriented methodologies, it empowers you to achieve financial success.

It is your responsibility as you are now focusing on providing and protecting a way of life for your family. Your values, attitudes and morals become the structure that greatly influences what you now do and how you now do it.

That was my message to the Blair family. They now had to take a new action to influence their financial future in a way that affects them right away: controlling their financial future.

It had to be my call to action to show them the impact that they can have on their lives. Please place yourself in the mindset of the Blair family.

They are working hard to provide and protect a way of life for their family. Their efforts seemed unrewarding and more too often, they were full of disappointments, a lack of any real savings and the things that just happen in life (water heater repair, car repair, children events).

Their debt total payments are $2,242 a month. When you add that to the household expenses, which total $2,608, they only had $150 remaining from their $5,000 net income each month. There's not much room here for change.

So, I ordered them to set the debt budget to minimum payments only. YES, I said minimum payments only. Mr. Blair asked me if I was out of my mind. He went on to say that every financial expert including the President has stated that making the minimum payments on a credit card is committing financial suicide.

He said, "Mr. Wilson, I am not going to put my family at risk. You talk a good game, Sir, but I do not see how making such a drastic move will protect my family."

You may be thinking the same thing here. How is this truly going to benefit his family over the long run? After all, there are countless stories, books and articles speaking highly against simply making the minimum payment.

I looked to his wife for support and she was looking at me as if I had become a great disappointment. She was my ally in this whole process.

I was in a "save (yourself, man) mode." "Wait," I said with passion. "We have been at this for some hours now. Each time that we hit a roadblock was for a purpose.

"Let me show you what you cannot see." I adjusted the current payments to the minimum payments and asked them to take a look now.

They saw these adjustments:

Debts	Minimum Payments	Balances
Credit Card 1	$280.00	$14,500.00
Credit Card 2	$220.00	$11,000.00
Credit Card 3	$167.00	$5,300.00
Credit Card 4	$100.00	$11,000.00
Credit Card 5	$125.00	$8,000.00
	$892.00	**$49,800.00**

They now see that their remaining income after paying all of their bills is now 10 times what they previously had each month. Yes, the new remaining income is now $1,500 each month.

It was a DUH moment. I redeemed myself only for a moment. Mr. Blair asked; "What do we do about the debt?" That was a legitimate question.

I said to him, "Now we begin to focus on creating wealth. This is where **Action Influence** becomes the tool to create the wealth mentality that I have been talking about.

First, like any family, we go through life chasing our dreams and our goals without a clearly defined purpose. What I want you to see the most is about creating purpose.

Carrying debt, living without a plan and not setting values will kill any ability to build wealth. Read what you should have learned.

Identify areas that you see you will have to work on. Use the planning process that I have talked about. Revisit information and points that really touched you.

Become very serious about your financial life. Decide to be different from the last time.

In the next chapter, I will show you how they eliminated all $49,800 of debt and created the foundation to build wealth.

A Motivational Quote

This is your time! Money, opportunities and possibilities have not left the planet. This is the time that you have to think on your feet. This is the time that you have to become relentless, unstoppable and carve out a place for yourself. Today you have to run just to stand still. Today you have to look ahead and anticipate things. Expect the unexpected and handle it.

This is your time! You must become focused, disciplined, consistent and unstoppable. Develop collaborative, achievement driven, productive relationships that will help you to work on your breakthrough. You have the power, ability and talent to create a new beginning. This is your time. Make it happen. You have something special! You have GREATNESS within you!

- Les Brown is a dynamic personality and highly-sought-after renowned motivational speaker.

What you should have learned in this chapter:

1. Not establishing and knowing your net income is a sure sign that you will fail.
2. The Blairs were able to change their mentality from poverty minded to wealth conscious.
3. It is critical for you to ask yourself serious questions.
4. Three areas that provide comfort and security for your family.
5. How to identify your home foundation (budget).
6. How you live becomes the blueprint of the foundation (budget).
7. When the core of your financial foundation (budget) is not in place, nothing else matters.
8. You have the ability to increase and move costs around, but you should never decrease.
9. The transitions from a poverty mindset to a wealth mentality.
10. As the manager of your home, you are able to establish a vision that allows you to view the process without risk.
11. No adjustment should be that dramatic and create such discomfort in the family.
12. This is about creating the foundation and having a wealth mentality.
13. How simple it was to set-up and manage their financial foundation (The Blair Family.)
14. Debt is like a cancer to your finances.
15. Making minimum payments only without a strategy can and will result in an endless attempt to get out of debt.
16. You must set goals that are relative to your family.
17. Every decision that you make has a cost.

18. Make a commitment to make wealth conscious decisions in every action of your life.
19. Determine the financial impact of all decisions made.
20. Secure the needs of your household, maintain a standard of living that suits you.
21. Most of the time, it comes down to our emotions and fear.
22. Our emotions can influence financial decisions in surprisingly predictable ways.
23. Consider that conscious thinking requires emotions, feelings and intuition.
24. Our spending behavior is guided by the influence of things that we are exposed to.
25. Our lack of sound money skills affects our ability to manage money.
26. **Action Influence** can give you a unique approach to achieving your financial goals.
27. A new action can influence your financial future in a way that affects you right away.
28. Your values, attitudes and morals become the structure that greatly influences what you now do and how you now do it.

Chapter 5

The Blair Family's Debt

Before I show you how the Blair family will pay off their debts, I want you to recapture the purpose of setting up your financial foundation (budget) as I discussed. It's about taking control of your financial life, changing the manner of how you manage your money and having a mentality to pursue wealth.

Once you create your financial foundation (budget), you will see that you have secured your lifestyle. How you and your family live every day has been reviewed and established. This is providing a way of life for your household.

I need to point out here that as you set up your financial foundation (budget), you must be clear in identifying the correct amount of net income.

Once the net income is determined and known, the financial foundation (budget) process becomes simple. You are no longer tracking your spending, you are establishing that way of life. **Please refer back to the questions in the last chapter.**

Remember, there are things about you and your family that are different from anyone else's household. However, there are many things that I am going to point out that may suit most households, like what type of food you eat each month. If you really think about your eating habits, you will find that you may be very consistent with your diet.

For example, I eat mostly fish and chicken each month, and there are at least three ways that I enjoy eating them. I enjoy blackened, baked, and fried fish on occasions. Sometimes, I really mix it up and prepare stir-fry dinners, eat white turkey meat, and a variety of grilled vegetables, along with rice or potatoes.

What you eat within your household daily is probably the most consistent meals that you consume each month. The key factors that matter the most here are your personal care, monthly entertainment, and cable service. These are all key factors that make most people comfortable within their own home.

The message I want you to get, the voice that I want you to hear is your own. There is a lifestyle standard for who you are, and for your family (secure that first). Be sure that you account for long-term savings and entertainment. If you are over doing it in some areas, make some adjustments.

However, I do not want you to devalue the quality of living for your household. I am using the term adjustments over cutbacks for a reason here. As we went over the Blair's story earlier, there were very little adjustments made. That does not mean that you will not have them.

Having your financial foundation (budget) complete, it is now time for you to begin to use it and get a good feel for how it can keep your finances in order.

Look at is this way, if there isn't any debt at all, the only thing you have left is your living and household expenses each month. What is that cost?

Think about it, your financial foundation (budget) consists of everything that runs your home. Secure your family and provide a way of life.

The Blair family household expenses are $2,603 each month. It provides them with entertainment, clothes, club fees, personal care, food, car repairs and insurance.

This is after the home expenses are secured and long-term savings are in place. Imagine this is your family with the same income and no debts at all. Imagine all of the financial security you would have.

The fact that your financial foundation (budget) allows you to prepare for the future, also allows you to forecast how much money you will be able to save for important things like your retirement. It is not about, "I deserve this," or even that you have earned it.

Now dealing with their debt situation is heavily on Mr. Blair's mind as it should be. A paradigm shift then becomes a source of relief when you have heavy burdens, or financial challenges that seem to overwhelm you.

This is where **Action Influence** really shows up and delivers. We have over $49,800 of credit card debt to eliminate.

There are things that I want you to consider before I walk you through the process that I want you to use. First, there are things that we did not concern ourselves with at all:

We did not consider:

Balances
Interest Rate
Type of credit cards

They were not told the following:

Cut up the credit cards
Cut back on expenses
Commit to using your "raise" to paying off debt
Contact creditors and negotiate lower rates
Use eBay to sell stuff around the house
Post your debt free goal on the fridge
Get a part- time job

I know that these are things that you have heard before. For years, most of my colleagues have used this approach and they are firm with this particular advice. I am approaching this completely differently by using what I believe is a stronger approach.

All of those things are important, necessary and possibly effective when your only goal is to become debt free. Being debt free is not a part of our focus.

In fact, time was our focus. It was what we needed to accomplish our overall goal. In this book, I have talked about things that provide a way of living for your family, your household and your future.

My approach with the Blair family is effective when the mentality of the person shifts from poverty to wealth-consciousness. It is important for you to understand the shift and the approach that I am providing you.

Remember earlier in chapter one, I mentioned that being poverty minded is the major factor that stops you from accumulating wealth and thinking positive in the terms of wealth accumulation. Those methods that I just pointed out lean more to the poverty side of things.

Moving from a poverty consciousness to a wealth-consciousness can be a never-ending challenge to transitioning from your old lifestyle to your new lifestyle. You can have a vision and goals while finding yourself getting deeper into debt or not saving any money.

These are stories I hear often. Thus, I write this book in hopes of making your life just a little easier, or, at the very least, help you to kick those poverty habits.

Perhaps some of you may be in a rapid downward spiral. You are willing to try anything to feel better and to do better financially. That does not matter if you are committed to gaining as much wealth information as you can.

That being said, like any new adjustment to your life, there will almost always be obstacles knocking at your door and waiting around every corner that you turn.

Transitioning your life will certainly test your abilities to stay committed and determined to WIN (Wealth Increasing Now).

Remember their debt situation while they were making huge additional payments on each of their credit cards. Once I required them to go back to the minimum payment only, it provided a substantial amount of remaining income.

Mr. Blair was concerned about getting out of debt and Mrs. Blair was thinking of shopping for a new kitchen. Even with me sitting there before them, they saw this $1,500 in a totally different way.

This is a normal reaction when additional money is made available. It is like a windfall; it becomes a reason or an excuse to go shopping. Here $1,500 came by way of budgeting and adjustments. It could come in the form of a raise, a tax refund, a generous birthday check or paying off a debt. Splurging can be fun, but that is not the best use of your money.

Be careful not to start feeling deprived and that you have to do something for yourself. This is one of the quickest ways to fall back into that poverty mentality: the feeling that you owe it to yourself. The mission here is for you to WIN (Wealth Increasing Now).

As I move forward with this process, you are going to see money grow. Using the same approach in your home can deliver you the very same results.

Okay we know that there is $1,500 of remaining income. However, I am only going to show you what we did with only $700. We will come back to the other $800. Now I want to deal with the debt.

Let's look at their debts again below:

Debts	Minimum Payments	Balances
Credit Card 1	$280.00	$14,500.00
Credit Card 2	$220.00	$11,000.00
Credit Card 3	$167.00	$5,300.00
Credit Card 4	$100.00	$11,000.00
Credit Card 5	$125.00	$8,000.00
	$892.00	**$49,800.00**

The very first thing that I had to make clear with them is that when we/you create this plan today, it must be complete and have a final date. When you plan a fun vacation, you know when the flight leaves and returns; you also know where you will be staying throughout the vacation, and you should know how much money you will have to spend.

This is a fun retirement planning party, you are going to know your debt elimination date, savings and investment dates, and most of all how much wealth you would have accumulated.

How is it possible that most people who struggle financially seem to have details on how to make ends meet? They are diligent in pursuing things that seem to keep them behind or deeper in debt.

Well let's get started with the debt elimination process. As I mentioned before, the Blair family's household budget is set in stone. Their lifestyle should include committment to a financial foundation (budget) that was set for them. All of their expenses have been identified and the appropriate amount is established.

With the $700 that they have committed to eliminating debt, a plan of action was created. We determined that the money to pay off debt would be saved each month as they continue to make regular minimum monthly payments on the debts.

One thing to remember is that each payment towards the debt in the budget reduces the total amount owed.

Debts	Minimum Payments	Balances
Credit Card 1	$280.00	$14,500.00
Credit Card 2	$220.00	$11,000.00
Credit Card 3	$167.00	$5,300.00
Credit Card 4	$100.00	$11,000.00
Credit Card 5	$125.00	$8,000.00
	$892.00	**$49,800.00**

The debts on the previous page are the debts they will eliminate over the next 44 months. There are five steps to this and each of them requires time. They first determined the foundation of the plan of action to eliminate the debt. Mr. Blair asked how they were going to pay off this amount of debt in just 44 months.

He stated that he had already done the math and if you took $700 x 44 months, you would get $30,800. My calculation was about $19,000 short of the goal that I set. "Where are we going to get the kind of money? Should we just use all of the remaining $1,500?" he asked.

I told him that he must work with the purpose of creating wealth. If the total amount of $1,500 is used, he would not have the financial freedom that I have discussed. I asked him to follow me as I set the new purpose for his finances. I want you to pay close attention here as well.

In setting up the plan to eliminate this debt, there must be a commitment to stay the course. Looking at the five credit cards, I determined that we would use what some call the snowball approach. I calculated and divided 5,300 / 700 = 7. This gave us our first payoff date.

That meant that the Blairs would continue to make regular minimum payments for six months on credit card 3. On the seventh month, they would take the $4,900 and add the minimum payment of $167. That would give them a total of $5,067 to pay off debt #1, considering that a portion of the minimum payments made over six months had reduced the balance on Credit Card 3.

Here is an important tip. As I create the plan, continue to use the balance amount of the plan's creation date. Over time, it will give you an advantage as you work to eliminate the debt.

As with any snowball effect, the minimum payment that was being paid towards debt remains as a part of the debt reduction process. Watch what happens here. So, now the $167 is added to the $700 that is for debt elimination, which now gives them a total of $867 to attack debt.

Now, they set a plan for Credit Card 5 using the same process: saving $867 for nine months. This gives them a total of $7,803 plus the monthly payment of $125 that gives them a total of $7,928 to pay off debt # 2. I explained to Mr. Blair that they are now in the 16th month of the 44-month plan. The plan so far has them eliminating **$13,300.**

I will say that this is a lot of credit card debt. Most of you will not have $1,500 a month of remaining income, neither will you have that amount of credit card debt. The process will still be the same regardless of the amount of debt or remaining income. I took 46% of the remaining income to start this process.

Regardless of your remaining income always use between 40% - 48% of that amount. This will give you an adequate amount of resources to do other things later. I will explain this more as we move forward.

Continue with the snowball effect, the minimum payment that was being paid towards debt #2 remains a part of the debt reduction process. Watch what happens here. So, now the $125 is added to the $867 that is for debt elimination, which now gives them a total of $992 to attack debt.

Setting the plan for Credit Card 2 using the same process, they will save $992 for 11 months a total of $10,912 plus the monthly payment of $220. That gives them a total of $11,132 to pay off debt # 3.

That is more than enough to pay the original balance amount, keeping in mind that over the 27 months of minimum payments, the balance may be alot lower.

Mr. Blair is smiling now. He is beginning to feel comfortable about the process. However, he still has his eyes on the other $800, wondering why we are not talking about it yet. Remember, this is simply the beginning stage of the debt reduction.

This is an important step towards a better financial life. Once you fully understand where you are currently, you can consider looking at your personal net worth. One of the steps to dramatically change your personal net worth is to move in a positive direction by decreasing debt.

Again, we are continuing with the snowball effect. The minimum payment that was being paid towards debt #3 remains as a part of the debt reduction process. So, now the $220 is added to the $992 that is for debt elimination, which now gives them a total of $1,212 to attack debt.

By setting the plan for Credit Card 4 using the same process, they will save $1,212 for eight months. This is a total of $9,696. Plus, the monthly payment of $100 gives a total of $9,796 to pay off debt # 4.

Finally, we are setting a plan for their final credit card debt to be completely eliminated. Nothing in the process or focus has changed. It took us about 20 minutes to set in stone a plan to eliminate their debts.

With the snowball effect, the minimum payment that was being paid towards debt #4 remains as a part of the debt reduction process. So, now the $100 is added to the $1,212 that is for debt elimination, which now gives them a total of $1,312 to attack this final debt.

Please remember when I created this plan that whatever the balance was on the plan creation date, I continued to use that balance amount. Over the entire time, only minimum payments were made to the balance.

Setting the plan for credit card 1, the final credit card debt, using the same process that they started with, they will save $1,312 for nine months.

A total of $11,808 plus the monthly payment of $280 gives a total of $12,088 to pay off debt # 5. They now have a complete 44-month debt elimination plan. It looked like this:

Pay-off Order	Number of Months	Balances
Debt # 5	9 Months	$14,500.00
Debt # 3	11 Months	$11,000.00
Debt # 1	7 Months	$5,300.00
Debt # 4	8 Months	$11,000.00
Debt # 2	9 Months	$8,000.00
Totals	**44 Months**	**$49,800.00**

Mr. Blair really is happy now that he can see a set plan in place to eliminate debt. On the other hand, Mrs. Blair is the one that has trouble with the plan. She wanted to know what she could do if something happened. She went on to say that things seem to have gone wrong every time they tried to do something that would benefit the family.

She is right; something will happen as it always does. The best plan of action is to do what we just completed. I want you to think about what I did with the Blair family. We first had a conversation about their income. This family fortunately had a great understanding of their net income and deduction. Most families may struggle in that area, which is why earlier in the book we talked about understanding your income.

Having a complete view of your net income is critical in the process of creating wealth. Knowing that your income is not your wealth, your income can allow you to accumulate wealth.

88

The very first element of **budgeting** is knowing your *Net Income*, Which is the amount of money you receive per a given timeframe (daily, weekly, monthly, etc.)

Income takes various forms: some are simple while others are complicated; some are regular, others are not. A few are one-time windfalls, while still others come in small streams. It differs with every individual as I described previously and there are different methods of calculating it. You may need to go back to page 42 and read the section on net income.

The next thing that we did here was to create a cost to their lifestyle. Remember I asked them to tell me their story. That series of questions gave them a realistic view on how they live each month. The answers to those questions with a realistic cost associated with those answers created their financial foundation (budget).

After creating that financial foundation (budget), I identified a process to eliminate their debts. By using the process of minimum payments, it freed up cash to be used for debt reduction and savings.

All of this action allows you to be in the strongest position possible to provide a way of life and protect your way of life. The next stage is to preserve that way of life for your family.

What you should have learned is this chapter:

1. Once you create your financial foundation (budget), you will see that you have secured your lifestyle.
2. Remember, there are things about you and your family that is so different from anyone else's household.
3. In your household, what you eat each month is probably the most consistent thing that you do.
4. Your personal care, monthly entertainment and cable service makes you comfortable within your home.
5. You do not want to devalue the quality of living for your household.
6. Think about it, your financial foundation (budget) consists of everything that runs your home, secures your family and provides a way of life.
7. The fact that your financial foundation (budget) allows you to prepare for the future also allows you to forecast how much money you will be able to save for important things like your retirement.
8. Being debt free is not a part of our focus.
9. Being poverty minded is the major factor that stops you from accumulating wealth and thinking positively in terms of wealth accumulation.
10. Moving from a poverty consciousness to a wealth-consciousness can be a never-ending challenge to transitioning from your old lifestyle to your new.
11. Just as you plan a fun vacation, you plan a fun retirement planning party.
12. Whatever the balances are on the plan creation date, continue to use that balance amount. The minimum payment should be paid towards debt as a part of the debt reduction process.

Chapter 6

The Blair Family's Savings

Preserving your way of life requires you to evaluate the reason that you must save. It is not optional; saving is and should be an absolute part of your daily life. This is one of the reasons that most people are very disappointing to me as a financial coach.

Most people need very little motivation to save for items that add no financial value to their homes or their lives. I can remember when a desktop computer costed $1,000, one of my clients told how they saved for six months to purchase one.

They were justifying that they knew how to save money. Yet, there was only $50 in their savings account some six months later.

Many financial experts agree that consumers should aim to have three to six months' living expenses saved for emergencies. They strongly believe that saving money is the cornerstone of paying for future financial goals.

These financial goals change as you move through life. It could be buying a home, buying a car, your college education or your children's college education.

People often feel as if they are under so much pressure to save money. They hear that there are so many reasons to begin saving money. Because of such pressure, people save for different reasons.

Amazingly, those reasons are short-term and do not provide the resources that were intended. There are plenty of reasons why people choose to save. I have listed six of the most common:

Save for a new car or vacation
Save for a down payment on a house
Save for luxury items
Save for emergency funds
Save for sinking funds
Save for education or for retirement

I am by no means stating that those reasons are not good ones. How about approaching saving in an **Action Influence** way as I have described? Create a savings that will provide you all of these things along with wealth to transfer.

Let me quickly point out that saving alone will not produce wealth. I will talk a great deal about moving from saving to investing in order to create wealth.

For now, let me focus on saving money. Mrs. Blair is nervous with this next process because it is not clear to her what I am asking them to do now.

Remember, in her eyes, she sees $800 that she can do some things with. Is it funny that she can see this money now, but couldn't see it before I rearranged her finances?

You will have this same experience. You will put your numbers down as they are. Then you will refocus with a plan of **Action Influence** and identify income that you should save.

In the preface of this book I mention this statement, "It is simply about learning how putting all of **your eggs in one basket** can make a difference in building wealth." I now want to walk you through that process.

PUTTING ALL YOUR EGGS IN ONE BASKET!

When I talk about putting all of your eggs into one basket, many of my colleagues get upset. This is not something that they teach and most people firmly believe that we should not have all of our eggs in one basket. This is why a paradigm shift is required to accomplish the wealth accumulation desired.

Let's explore just some of the reasons that they teach this bad concept.

Are you putting all of your eggs in one basket?

• **Do you have all of your money in the stock market?**
• **Do you have all of your money in your savings account?**
• **Do you have all of your money in fixed-income investments?**

If you answered "yes" to any of these questions, you are seriously endangering your financial health. A smart financial plan starts with diversification - allocating your assets among several investment classes.

For example, after gauging your risk tolerance, you should distribute your savings among high-risk investments such as stocks, low-risk investments such as bonds and liquid investments such as money market accounts. Diversity is the key to protecting your savings.

THIS IS WHAT THEY TEACH.

Do not **risk everything on one endeavor.** It is less risky to have more than one investment. There is a story about a man that put all of his eggs in the same basket, which was buying gold. Therefore, when the price of gold dropped, he lost everything.

What a disaster! You do not want to put yourself at risk. I am sure that his purpose for buying gold as an investment was to reach financial security at some point. Now, it is gone.

It is said that all of your money should not go into the bank. Even if there is a guarantee to secure your money up to $250,000 by the FDIC, you should not do it.

The main reason is that you will never get rich or build wealth with your money in a bank. It does not pay enough interest. What is 1.5 %?

The real goal is establishing financial independence. Most people who only put their money in a single investment portfolio are very much at a higher risk level than others.

The idea that you put everything (all of your eggs) in one basket just seems scary. Some would say that if you (the market) fall down they would all crack (you lose all).

If financial independence is your goal, it must have some form of diversity. One problem I think that I really need to discuss is that they always relate diversity to investors. *That is major for me. Why should diversity only be connected to a slogan called investors*?

Sometimes it seems that everywhere you go, you hear people talking about themselves as one of them. An investor is defined as someone who puts their money in stocks and bonds. Some are also are known to put their money into real estate.

These people work hard not to put all of their eggs in just one single basket. The objective of an investor is to obtain the largest possible rate of return without placing invested funds at more risk than is bearable.

The reluctance to assume risk limits your ability to maximize returns. You should not assume the risk of a greater loss than you can afford. The basic idea: **maximize returns and minimize risks.**

You are looking for a return. Just what is a return on an investment? I think you should know. **Return = Money You Gain.**

I want you to consider that the rate of return is the most important outcome from any investment. Both the gain in an asset's value over time (the capital gain) and the monies received while holding an asset (the cash dividend) is of interest to you.

If you add the cash you receive in hand (like interest payments and dividends) together with any capital gain and divide it by the purchase price, you then know the true return on your money.

Capital Gain (or loss)
+ Cash Dividend / Purchase Price

= THE RETURN ON YOUR INVESTMENT

You want to accomplish this with minimum risk. I will talk more about this in the next chapter, along with putting all of your eggs in one basket.

Now that the debt elimination plan is created, it is time to establish a plan for saving. The purpose is to preserve the way of life for your family. The Blair family had $200 going into their savings each month as a part of the financial foundation (budget).

It is important for them to identify this savings as long-term savings. By having the long-term savings, they are learning to expect the unexpected. This prevents a minor financial setback from turning into a major financial crisis.

That alone is not enough. With the remaining $800, I instructed them to do a number of things that made them feel comfortable. First, I divided the $800 into four parts with $200 going to long-term savings, giving it a total of $400 a month.

I suggested they both needed to create a savings account and place $200 in each account each month. That means that both Mr. Blair and Mrs. Blair would open individual savings accounts. They had to place the final $200 into a household savings account that would serve as medium to long-term savings.

Mr. Blair was quick to point out that they may find themselves going into those savings accounts from time to time. I immediately asked him if he would really need to.

Did you not account for entertainment, personal care, clothes, gas and food in your financial foundation (budget)? What will you need this money to do?

This will be a challenge if there is not a shift in thinking. The whole purpose of creating a financial foundation (budget) is to secure life. I had to take them back to the beginning of the process and remind them that they were making debt payments with this money.

Mrs. Blair asked, "What is the plan with this money? Are we to just save it?" She asked that question as if saving money was a waste of time.

You are going to have to be very careful not to lose track of your goals. **Action Influence**: I cannot say that enough. I had to work quickly to show them the plan with this money.

I started by asking them about the debt reduction and elimination plan that we set. "How many months will it take you to pay off the debt?" They replied only 44 months.

Then let's talk about your car payment for a minute. The Blairs mentioned they have two years of payments remaining on the car.

"Great," I said. "Over the next 24 months as you work to pay off the car with the regular payment in your financial foundation (budget), I want you to start saving every remaining penny as I just laid out for you."

Long-Term Savings in (budget) is now $400 each month x 24 months will = $9,600

Medium to Long-Term savings is $200 a month x 24 month will = $4,800

The **Two Combined Personal Savings** is $400 a month x 24 months will = $9,600

"If you save this money as I laid out over the 24-month period, you will have saved a total of $24,000." Mr. and Mrs. Blair just looked at each other.

Mrs. Blair immediately said, "Something is going to happen and we will have to use this money." Yes, something may happen, but the biggest thing that should happen is your new course of **Action Influence.**

I told them, "Just as we set the plan for the debt elimination, I set the savings plan over the same period. Now that your car has been paid off and the payment of $350 is available. I want you to save it as well."

This could be a great challenge or a major success for your family. Most people would go and buy another car or new furniture because this money is available.

The poverty mentality is knocking on the door. As you are reading this, you may have come up with some options on how to use that $350 yourself.

I told the Blairs that I needed them to complete the savings plan for the next 20 months. This will give them a total savings plan that will be completed at the same time as the debt elimination. Remember, I am setting up all three of the plans for this family all on the same day.

I would demand that you set up your plans in the same manner. It will give you control and focus. It will also help you stay on the path of wealth-consciousness.

The ability to see what you can accomplish with your money and secure your household at the same time is priceless.

These are the results that developed over the next 20 months:

Long-Term Savings in (budget) is now $400 each month x 20 months will = $8,000

Medium to Long-Term savings is $200 a month x 20 month will = $4,000

Two Combined Personal Savings is $400 a month x 20 months will = $8,000

Former Car Payment was $350 a month x 20 months will = $7,000

In just 44 months, the Blair family will pay off $49,800 in credit cards and $8,400 on a car note. That equals $58,200. In that same period, they will save $51,000.

This is a powerful example of how **Action Influence** shifts the mentality from poverty to wealth. As I set up these plans for the Blair family, I had only the three reasons from the very beginning: Provide, Protect and Preserve.

If you are mired in debt to where you cannot think of saving, you should not despair. Just as I created this debt repayment plan, it helped us to identify and eventually free up financial resources to save for the future.

As with any good savings plan, there must be regular contributions, not just a single or periodic attempt to save.

A Motivational Quote

Be good to yourself. Do something for you for a change. Give yourself a special treat. Do something that brings you a sense of joy ~ either spending time alone or with someone...or doing something that you like that excites you. Ask yourself some thought provoking questions that will help the next chapter be the best chapter of your life.

What are three things that I can do each day that can make me proud of myself?

What are five things I'm grateful for?

What does the next chapter of my life look like?

What do I want at this point in my life?

What makes me happy?

Give yourself permission to check out from all the things that could possibly stress you. Allow yourself the time to reconnect with yourself, your heart and your spirit.

You have one precious life. Make it a point to actually enjoy it. Live it. Remember, you have something special. You have GREATNESS within you!!

- Les Brown is a dynamic personality and highly-sought-after renowned motivational speaker.

What you should have learned in this chapter:

1. Preserving your way of life requires you to evaluate the reason that you must save.
2. It is not optional. Saving is and should be an absolute part of your daily life.
3. Approach saving in an **Action Influence** way.
4. The real goal is establishing financial independence.
5. Saving alone will not produce wealth.
6. If financial independence is your goal, it must have some form of diversity.
7. It is important for the Blairs to identify this savings as long-term savings.
8. By having the long-term savings, they are learning to expect the unexpected.
9. A minor financial setback should not turn into a major financial crisis.
10. You should have a household savings account that would serve as medium to long-term savings.
11. Start saving every remaining penny.
12. **Action Influence** shifts the mentality from poverty to wealth.

13. The whole purpose of creating a financial foundation (budget) is to secure life.
14. Creating a debt repayment plan will help to identify and eventually free up financial resources to save for the future.
15. Something may happen, but the biggest thing that should happen is your new course of **Action Influence**.
16. Stay on the path of wealth-consciousness.

The ability to see what you can accomplish with your money and secure your household at the same time is priceless.

Chapter 7

Eggs in a Basket

Wow! In this chapter, you may get confused. I am going to discuss what I instructed the Blair family to do with their savings and to move toward investing. To do this effectively, they (you) have to understand risk in a wealth mentality rather than a poverty mentality.

What I intend to do here is give you another perspective to create a stronger financial foundation (savings) that not only guides you in the process of creating wealth but also makes you financially stronger in dealing with financial concerns.

Most households are unbanked or under banked, meaning that their financial relationship with the bank is at a minimum, in which they have no banking facilities at all, or they have poor access to mainstream financial services normally offered by retail banks.

They have a strong reliance on non-traditional forms of finance and micro-finance often associated with the disadvantaged and the poor, such as check cashing facilities, loan sharks and pawnbrokers.

There is also that growing segment that is not actively engaged in the use of traditional banking products. They are using Pre-Paid cards believing that it helps them to build financial independence. This is not your journey. This is a poverty mentality that I am trying to eliminate in everyone that I touch.

Do not be fooled. This is not limited to low-income households. To the contrary, many households, regardless of income, find themselves with credit challenges or fear of using banks, which is why they end up using Pre-Paid cards.

I do not want to leave out the many households that are afraid of banking fees. So many households do not use banks because of the many fees that are required to maintain a basic account.

They are using money orders in lieu of cash or checks to pay monthly expenses or utility bills and to meet their needs. This chapter is going to answer all of these concerns.

Why Save or Invest?

I asked the Blair family that question. The answer was always to get a return on their money. So, is this really all about getting a return? Then, what is wrong with that, you might ask? Nothing at all, it seems.

But, the amount of return is based on the measure of risk. The higher the risk, the greater the return. Or, the lower the risk, the lower the return.

Most people are averse to risk, giving it the name risk-aversion. For instance, when you buy a publicly traded stock, you could lose your entire investment.

On the other hand, if you did not invest in the stock market during certain periods of history, you would have forgone huge profits. That is called profit-aversion. To be totally risk-averse or totally risk-tolerant does not appear to be the best investment strategy. So, what we are looking for is a sane approach to risk management.

Risk

Assets having a greater probability of loss are felt as "more risky" than those with a lesser chance of loss. The trick is getting the greatest rate of return with the least amount of risk.

A common approach to evaluating the risk of an asset involves estimating the pessimistic (worst), the most likely (expected) and the optimistic (best) return associated with a given asset. If you take a group of investments and plot the estimated risk against the return, it usually looks like this:

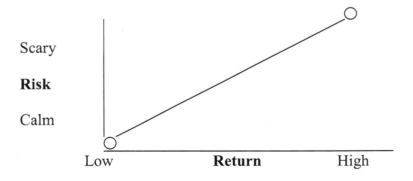

Well, we looked at returns on investment as well as the risks associated with investing and the one key is...*Diversification*. They say you should never put your eggs into one basket?

In order to reduce overall risk (the steepness of the above graph), it is best to acquire, or add to the existing portfolio, assets that are not related. The technical term for this is not putting all your eggs in one basket. **That way if you trip, you won't break all the eggs.**

Now, let's translate that over to your money: The creation of a portfolio by combining two assets that behave exactly the same way cannot reduce the portfolio's overall risk below the risk of the least risky asset. (Here comes the important part.)

The creation of a portfolio by **combining two or more assets that behave exactly opposite can** reduce the portfolio's total risk to a level below that of either asset alone, which, in certain situations, may be zero.

Now, you want to build wealth, right? **Combining two or more assets that behave exactly opposite** is one of the strategies that I believe support putting all of your eggs into one basket.

Let us look at this in another way. I hope that you have read the entire story of the Blair family and how I worked to change their thinking. That process was about changing your mentality from things associated with poverty to wealth. Likewise, you must change your views about your finances.

In Chapter 5, you were able to see how we eliminated debt and were able to save a lot of money. Many people always ask me what they should do with the $50,000 that is now saved.

Remember, I said earlier that the basic idea of **maximizing returns, minimizing risks and accumulating assets** are the keys to creating wealth. Well, the real question that I think you should ask is this. What do I really want in my financial life? If the answer is financial freedom, let's take a look at it.

I believe that most people who really begin to pursue financial freedom are faced with a lot of credit challenges, either currently or from their past.

Credit challenges create a real negative atmosphere of risk in your financial life. The reason given to not put all of your eggs into one basket is because of the risk involved.

Even if you are not credit challenged, you may not have fully utilized your financial potential. Your mortgage is probably with a bank that you have never heard of.

The car loan that you need is being shopped to all types of lenders for financing. That personal loan seems to be so far out of reach that you choose to use a title loan company.

These sources themselves make all of their profits because of the risks that create a return for them. I want you now to understand that you can play this same *G. A. M. E. (Gaining Assets Manage Effectively) and W. I. N. (Wealth Increasing Now)* at it. If money is being made due to risk, whether up or down, it creates an earning environment.

In your own world, you must see how you have put yourself at risk by not using the most basic tool or resources out there. The banking system can be used by you to reach your financial freedom goals. They carry the most basic and needed products to set you on the right path.

It also allows you to have what every investor tells you that is needed whenever you invest. In order to reduce overall risk, it is best to acquire or add to the existing portfolio assets that are not related.

The technical term for this is not putting all of your eggs in one basket. Is to called diversity: putting your money in different products by **combining two or more assets that behave exactly opposite**.

Now, it is time for you to behave exactly opposite of what you have done. Because your goals to financial freedom will not change, it is time to have opposite behavior from your past.

Think about this: for the most part, what I am about to share with you is probably something you have never completely done. Some of you may have done a couple of things but did not understand its value.

It is time now to eliminate all of the wasted efforts to do a simple thing and do it right. "Simple Process Creates Great Moments" - Rob Wilson

The bank offers you a lot of different products. Each of them are **assets that behave exactly opposite.** This becomes your new basket. Here is where you will accomplish many different things.

Your risk and the return due to your risk are now also changed. If you slip and fall, you now will have the ability to save all of your eggs.

Credit challenges will be completely eliminated. Your next mortgage, car loan or personal loans are easier obtained and at lower rates. Your ability to borrow money is greatly enhanced.

Financial freedom becomes a reality. You have to simply know how to play the **G. A. M. E.** (Gaining Assets Manage Effectively). Now you are in a position to **W. I. N.** (Wealth Increasing Now).

Mr. and Mrs. Blair are very excited about this discussion about money-making money. When I discussed getting a return on their money, they began to ask which stocks they were going to buy first.

As their coach, I had the responsibility to protect their next move. No stock purchasing right now; there is still a lot of work required to complete your financial foundation (savings).

I reminded them of this statement from Chapter 1, *"Every dollar that you have possession of can start the process of creating wealth. Remember that being poverty minded is the major factor that stops you from accumulating wealth and thinking positive in the terms of wealth accumulation."* The mission is to create wealth.

Now I will show you how we used the amount of money that was saved in Chapter 6 and how it can work for you. The actual grand total of savings is $51,000.

109

Keep in mind that this is your financial foundation (savings). They are about to create for the very first time a true financial fingerprint.

I will look at six banking products in this process that will give diversification. I will put equal amounts in each account to create a different financial picture. The purpose here is to change your financial foundation (savings) in order to build wealth.

This will be done by taking $7,000 and placing it in six different types of accounts at the bank. We will do so and look very briefly at possible returns.

First, to satisfy those of you who feel that you just have to invest in the stock market, I want you to see and enjoy this. There will be $9,000 left that will go into the stock market.

Let me get back to the money we have to go in the basket (bank). Purposely, you have to consider the products and the reason for using them.

We will put $7,000 in a bank account. It may draw or earn 1-2% interest on the account (the lower the risk the lower the return).

The purpose of using this bank account carries many reasons. First, you are now able to pay your monthly expenses before the bills come in each month.

This will create on time payment history for your credit history. Secondly, by choosing wisely, you can open up the right type of checking account that eliminates fees due to your average daily balance.

Thirdly, things will happen and you will need cash for emergencies. This account will be used for that purpose. Finally, any vacation and big-ticket items can come from this account. Please remember that your monthly saving will continue after this 44-month period.

Next, we use a **savings account** that may earn 2% to 3%. This savings account is the back up support to your checking account. It is also a part of your short to medium term financial goals. It is not for the purpose of dipping in and out because the money is available.

The next account will be a **money market account** that could earn 3%-5% interest. This account moves forward to create a stronger financial foundation for medium term goals. The purpose is to create the first line of personal investing, having money to liquidate at minimum risk.

There is a **certificate of deposit (CD)** that can possibly earn 4% +. If you really won't need the money for a while, lock it up for a longer term (within reason, a bank CD rate may not be the best return if your time horizon is greater than 5 years or so).

Also, see what interest rates are doing. If you think they are headed up, you may benefit by using a shorter term because bank CD rates will be more attractive in the future. Of course, it is *very* hard to predict interest rates and markets − don't knock yourself out trying to time it just right.

If you want to get the best rates, sometimes you have to meet certain minimums. If you have your assets spread out at various institutions, you may be missing out on "preferred customer" rates. There is an advantage to consolidating your assets at a given institution.

Then we have the **individual retirement account** (IRA), which could earn nearly 5% +. I really like this account because you can have a whole lot of diversity with it.

Considering a Roth IRA can be the long-term retirement account that contains investments in securities, usually common stocks and bonds, often through mutual funds. Sometimes you may find other investments, including derivatives, notes, certificates of deposit and real estate.

At most banks, they have a **brokerage account.** It gives you the ability to choose a lot of different products. This account allows you to purchase stocks, bonds, mutual funds and other investments by paying the banking professional to buy or sell the items you tell them to.

This, of course, could possibly bring you a much higher return, but it also comes with some higher risks. Now, imagine you in your current position with all the above things in one basket:

- What would your credit life be like?
- Who would you attempt to get your mortgage from?
- How differently could you go out to purchase your next car?
- Who could you possibly get a loan of any kind from?

These few things are just a small part of a bigger financial picture. By following the principles here in this book, the Blairs, over the next 44 months would be able to save over $102,000 and that is not counting what they already have in their basket. In closing, I really hope that you share with others that having all of your eggs in one basket is a good thing.

What you should have learned in this chapter:

1. Risk in a wealth mentality rather than a poverty mentality.
2. Reliance on non-traditional forms of finance and micro-finance are often associated with the disadvantaged and the poor.
3. Pre-Paid cards do not help you build financial independence.
4. Always get a return on your money.
5. The amount of return is based on the measure of risk.
6. The higher the risk, the greater the return. Or, the lower the risk, the lower the return.
7. A common approach to evaluating the risk of an asset involves estimating the pessimistic (worst), the most likely (expected) and the optimistic (best) return associated with a given asset.
8. The creation of a portfolio by **combining two or more assets that behave exactly opposite can** reduce the portfolio's total risk.
9. You must change your view about your finances.
10. Play this same **G. A. M. E.** (Gaining Assets Manage Effectively).
11. You can **W. I. N.** (Wealth Increasing Now) at it.
12. When money is being made due to risk, rather up or down, it creates an earning environment that must also become your environment.
13. You can reach your entire goals to financial freedom by using the banking system.
14. Diversity is putting your money in different products by **combining two or more assets that behave exactly opposite**.

15. "Simple Process creates Great Moments"
    – Rob Wilson
16. Credit challenges will be completely eliminated.
17. Your next mortgage, car loan or personal loans are easier and possibly much cheaper.
18. Your ability to borrow money is without question greatly enhanced.
19. Get excited about money-making money.
20. Every dollar that you have possession of can start the process of creating wealth.
21. The mission is to create wealth.
22. Change your financial foundation (savings) in order to build wealth.
23. Create on time payment history for your credit history.
24. Using a bank product as your basket or portfolio eliminates fees due to your average daily balance. Create the first line of personal investing by having money to liquidate at minimum risk.
25. There is an advantage to consolidating your assets at a given institution.

Chapter 8

The Blair Family's Investment

With all that was accomplished with the Blair Family, you could get the sense that it is enough. In fact, they are only half way in completing their financial goals for their future.

Knowing that they now have a good solid savings plan in place, it's important to consider a solid investment plan for long-term (retirement).

Both Mr. and Mrs. Blair started talking about their 401k plans that they have on their jobs. It was a very intense conversation.

They, like most households, believe that 401k investments are enough to fund your retirement. I had to make the case that it is not.

With both of them over the age of 40 and having not really started saving for retirement, making large annual contributions may not be enough to reach their retirement goals.

Their focus had been on paying off their debt more than saving for retirement. Does that sound familiar to you? When you consider retirement saving and investing, there are things that you need to determine.

1. How much can you expect from Social Security?
2. What other sources of income can you count on in retirement?
3. How much does your employer contribute to your 401k plan?
4. How much are you contributing to your 401k plan?
5. What kind of lifestyle do you want in retirement?

All of the above questions are critical in determining how much money you will need in retirement. Don't think that your 401k plan alone will be enough.

This is why we are putting together this financial plan. Regardless of your age, do not simply rely on your 401k plan alone. I am going to talk later about 401k and your advantages.

Mrs. Blair asked about her Roth Individual Retirement Account (IRA). She stated that she purchased an IRA three years ago for $5,000.

This was money from a settlement of some kind. Mr. Blair jumped in and said that it wasn't making them any money.

I laughed, and I then told them that based on the budget information and all of the numbers that we went over, there was never any mention of monthly contributions being made to the Roth.

Without making regular contributions, a single lump-sum investment, in an IRA account will have minimum growth. Do not get trapped here.

Listen, they are not alone. Most people try to do something about their financial goals. They will make the minimum contribution to their 401k and/or they will open up a Roth or some other type of investment product. This gives them the feeling or the gratitude that they are doing something.

Never consider or settle with the idea that you are trying or doing something. This is your future that you are working to secure.

How many times in your adult life have you said, at some point, that you wish that you were a certain age again to go back and do it over?

Trust me when I tell you that when your day of earning and making money is over, you do not want to look back and wonder, "What if?"

Live and prepare for your retirement dream now. What will your life be like when you have achieved your most deeply held dreams? What will your life be like when you retire? Start investing and living your retirement dreams this very day.

Ask yourself, do I have a retirement dream, a retirement vision of the life that I wish to live? How clear is that dream or vision? How do you intend to reach it?

There will be obstacles that might stand in your way. By creating the right enviroment you can change your circumstances. You can move beyond your present circumstances, beyond the challenges that come with change.

Without panic, this area of your financial goals should be your daily focus. This is why I am walking you through **Action Influence** from the beginning to your retirement.

Each phase or step is necessary. Mindset, behavior, action, consciousness, thought and influence all affect your money and your future.

Now that the Blair family has identified their income, they have set a workable budget for their household with long-term (retirement) savings included in that budget, a debt reduction plan and personal and investment savings in place. It is time to secure retirement.

As you may recall, we included long-term savings in their household budget. Once the budget and debt reduction was set, we increased the long-term savings from $200 to $400 a month. That became the overall long-term savings that totaled $17,600.

However, only $9,000 is going into the retirement savings portion. The remainder of that long-term savings was used as a part of the medium to long-term savings. I do not want to confuse you here. In the next chapter, I will go over all of the steps to bringing clarity to those numbers.

This $9,000 retirement started at the very beginning. That $200 long-term savings was set up into an investment portfolio according to their risk tolerance.

They looked at the S&P 500 (Standard and Poor 500 Index) and chose to invest $200 a month into a diversified portfolio that included a variety of products.

Doing this process gave them dollar cost averaging as they purchased stocks each month. What is dollar cost averaging?

It is a technique of buying a fixed dollar amount of a particular investment on a regular schedule, regardless of the share price. More shares are purchased when prices are low, and fewer shares are bought when prices are high.

Over this period, the average cost per share will become smaller and smaller. Dollar-cost averaging lessens the risk of investing a large amount in a single investment at the wrong time.

Our choice of using Standard & Poor 500 Index funds is available to you and would be low-cost, no-load, which are offered by many of the major mutual fund companies.

Before the advent of S&P 500 Index funds, first introduced by the Vanguard Group, the selection process would have definitely been more difficult.

We would have needed to select one or more investments from thousands of available securities and managed mutual funds. Being able to invest in an S&P 500 Index fund eliminates the need for this selection process.

As far as picking which stocks to buy, or even which mutual funds to buy, the advent of Standard and Poor 500 Index funds have reduced this to a no-brainer.

When you buy shares of a market index like a Standard and Poor 500 Index, you can expect to get the rate of return of the overall market.

The S&P 500 Index is composed of the stocks of the 500 largest companies in America and is said to represent 70 percent of the value of all U.S. traded common stocks.

The S&P 500 Index consistently outperforms all but a handful of managed mutual funds every year, and rarely does the same individual mutual fund continue to beat this index over any extended period of time.

A Standard and Poor 500 Index fund becomes a simple, easy solution to the challenge of selecting "the right" securities. No selection is required!

With this fund you will always be widely diversified in a broadly based cross section of the economy and should expect to prosper over the years to the same extent as our country prospers.

You won't have to worry about it! In no way, shape or form will you ever need to try to pick the perfect time to buy or sell your mutual fund shares. It's not necessary.

This is because you will use the investment approach called "dollar cost averaging," which means, you will regularly and automatically buy a fixed dollar amount of your fund every month or every pay period without regard to whether the price of these shares is up or down at the time you invest.

The "magic" of this approach is that your fixed dollar amount buys more shares when prices are lower and fewer shares when prices are higher, and you end up investing quite efficiently.

The average cost of your shares is favorably influenced by the fact that you automatically get more shares for your money when the market is down and fewer shares for the same amount of money when the market is higher.

You'll tell your banker or mutual fund company you want to automatically invest a regular dollar amount (such as the $200) every month into their S&P 500 Index fund, and they should debit your bank account for this amount monthly on whatever date you select.

The mutual fund company will have you complete some paperwork, forward your opening deposit and will set you up for a regular automatic investment.

This becomes a major part of your retirement plan. You are not eliminating your 401k or any other investment or savings. Just one more ingredient for your master retirement plan. Once you follow these steps, you are well on your way.

However, remember that true financial goals should be about financial security. Financial security is not limited to making or having a certain amount of money. There are many people who we have read about or seen that, at one point in their lives, they made millions of dollars.

Today, they are not financially secure. It is not about life-styles of the rich and famous reality shows that you see on the networks.

I have to say that it is not about being or becoming debt free. As I stated earlier, a homeless man is debt free and he does not have or pursue wealth-accumulating assets.

This journey of Wealth Increasing Now and the road to financial security is about setting financial goals and taking control of savings, not spending.

Controlling your savings and investing creates the environment that your spending is choked off. The overwhelming result is the accomplishments toward your financial security.

Before you complete this book, I want you to do a few surveys. These surveys are very important for your personal financial growth.

The first survey is with your family. I want you to ask two members of your family three questions. Once they answer the questions jot down their answers. Even if you think you know their answers before you ask the question, still complete the survey.

1. What do you think about wealth?
2. Has there ever been a transfer of wealth in your family?
3. Do you think that you will transfer wealth?

Second, ask three of your co-workers.
1. Do you think that your income can create wealth?
2. Do you think that you can retire from this job?
3. Do you think you will ever return to work after retirement?

Finally, when you are out with some friends or maybe call at least two of them and ask them the following.
1. Has wealth ever been transferred in your family?
2. Will your job provide you with enough for retirement?
3. What are you doing for retirement savings?

Once you complete the survey, I want you to review the answers that everyone has given you. Then compare them to how you were thinking prior to reading the book. Compare it to your thinking now. If there is not a huge difference, start over with the book and get serious.

This is how you are going to define your own purpose to financial security. Financial security is an admirable goal. The **Action Influence** that you take makes it achievable.

What you should have learned in this chapter:

1. You must have a good solid savings plan in place.
2. It is important to consider a solid investment plan for long-term (retirement).
3. Your 401k investments are not enough to fund your retirement.
4. Making large annual contributions may not be enough to reach your retirement goals.
5. When you consider retirement savings and investing, there are things that you need to determine.
6. Without making regular contributions and with just a single lump-sum investment, the Roth account will have minimum growth.
7. Never consider or settle with the idea that you are trying or doing something.

8. Mindset, behavior, action, consciousness, thought and influence all affect your money and your future.
9. Dollar cost averaging is buying a fixed dollar amount of a particular investment on a regular schedule, regardless of the share price.
10. Dollar-cost averaging lessens the risk of investing a large amount in a single investment at the wrong time.

Chapter 9

The Blair Family's Summary

Now let's review and go over some of the fine details of your financial foundation. The first thing that was required for the Blair family was to create a real eye opening experience. The best way to get them to refocus and categorize their lifestyle was to simply ask them to discuss their lifestyle.

But, before they really got a chance to discuss their financial situation, I talked to them about wealth and poverty, the mindset (mentality) and the consciousness. I discussed how real wealth is accumulated over time.

The fact is that wealth does not come by some financial masterstroke, marrying into money or obtaining it through an inheritance or luck.

It's not by winning the lottery, getting into the "right" stock or business on the ground floor or just being lucky enough to know the right people at the right time. Situations like these can jump-start your wealth-building program.

This is not how most wealthy people get that way. In fact, coming into lots of money quickly before learning how to manage it can actually be hazardous to your wealth building.

There must be a mindset transformation, however, before wealth is accumulated you must refocus on what you think you know about money. There must be a conscious effort to evolve with Financial Ethics.

Having Financial ETHICS is the fundamental steps to achieving wealth. The patience and commitment that is required is the difficult part. (See Chapter One)

For many people, the word "budget" has a negative connotation. Instead of thinking of a budget as financial handcuffs, think of it as a means to achieve your highest financial success.

Setting financial goals is important. Any financial goal set should expand beyond life goals. Let me explain that briefly.

Any true financial goals set must consider wealth transfer, sustaining life, retirement and financial freedom.

That fancy car, television, mp3, iPhone, vacation, education and any other big-ticket item is really not as important.

Whether you make thousands of dollars a year or over hundreds of thousands of dollars a year, a budget is the first and most important step you can take towards putting your money to work for you instead of being controlled by it and forever falling short of your financial goals.

The goal is for you to build and create wealth for your future and the future of your children's children. A foundation that is established correctly will allow you to grow and expand. Setting up the financial foundation (budget), should be your last financial foundation.

This is not about just getting help or looking to change your money habits when you want something.

You want to try to eliminate credit card debt.
You want to save for a new car.
You want to go on vacation.
You want to pay for college tuition.
You want to buy your first house.

My main point is all about elevating your thinking. This is the time for you to really evaluate your own mentality and determine where you are.

That is the one thing that I could not do or give them. I did give them reasons to help them move forward with a wealth consciousness rather than the poverty-conscious mentality.

For most households, spending is the largest concern. However, I believe that not knowing your net income total each month is the largest problem.

So, I asked them about their net income. By identifying the net income, they are now able to effectively begin to organize their household. Then we talked about their family and how they live.

There were many questions that were asked and talked about.

What does your family do, or like to do each month for fun?
What do you do for personal care?
How often do you buy clothes?
Do you belong to any type of club where there is a fee?
Is your car new or used and do you have a payment for it?
Do you have any car maintenance?
Do you have many miles to drive during the week?
How many cell phones do you have?
How often do you go grocery shopping monthly? Why is that?
Do you have any type of insurance you are paying directly?
Are there any other children outside of the marriage that you are responsible for or that someone else is responsible to you?
Are you a family of faith? If so, do you pay tithes and offerings?
Are you buying your home?
Are you able to keep your lights and utilities paid regularly?
Do you have any credit cards?
Are you paying them each month?
Are you making the minimum payments on them all? If so, may I ask why?
What is the total amount of all of your credit card debt?
What is the lowest interest rate on one of your cards?
Are you saving money now?

What I did with the Blair family was identify their home foundation (budget). When you are setting up your foundation, it will take a little work.

Instead of tracking what they (you) are spending, they (you) begin with how they (you) live. How they (you) live becomes the blueprint of the foundation (budget). Each week they (you) may eat out for lunch, which can range from $15 a week or more to do so.

Once a month they (you) may enjoy going to the movies
with the family. That may cost $50 along with popcorn and
sodas. This routine can establish an entertainment cost of
$110 a month.

This is what I wanted the Blair family to see and for you to
realize. There were three areas that must be secured at all
times. (See Chapter Two) This is the family vanguard
(standard of living).

There will be an opportunity and the ability to increase
it/move costs around, but you should never decrease it. That
changes your family's lifestyle. This is your foundational
position that allows everything else to happen.

Be mindful that reasonable cutbacks are okay. You should
not have to give up your home, your car or reduce your living to eating beans and rice. Getting your expenses set on
budget billing or reducing your entertainment and personal
care is a start.

This is where I needed them (you) to experience the transition from a poverty mindset to a wealth mentality. It will
have you feeling the need to get quick results. There is nothing wrong with that as long as the foundation is set and your
goals are clear.

So we began to set their numbers; real numbers to answer the
questions that I previously asked. I asked them to tell me a
story about their family, their life and how they live. This is
how I communicated back to them.

So, you stated that you occasionally go out for dinner, enjoy going to the movies, ice skating and your son is involved in school sports.

Eating out $75, Ice skating $35, the movies $30

Getting your hair done and basic personal hygiene. Personal care $75 Seasonal clothing $75

The kids (Chess & tennis) club fees. $300 a year.

Your car payment is $350 a month. Your maintenance is $25 a month.

Gas for your car is $80, the cable bill is $45, your cell phone is $75 Your food cost is $250

Your car insurance $100 a month and life insurance $38 a month.

You pay tithes and offerings $200

You are buying your home $785

Your lights is $50, your gas is $50 your water and sewer is $25

The balance on credit cards is:

Credit Card 1 $14,500.00
Credit Card 2 $11,000.00
Credit Card 3 $5,300.00
Credit Card 4 $11,000.00
Credit Card 5 $8,000.00

Total debt is $49,800

You are saving $175 every month.

This is how all of the numbers look as they provided them to me. Of course, I made some changes.

This is the moment that they (you) can claim and begin to see a road to prosperity. It all begins with how they (you) manage what they (you) currently have.

The desire for more comes when you are not taking care of what you have. It really puts you in that "I'm ready to be deceived mode". That poverty mentality has held you back for too long.

As the manager of your home, you are able to establish a vision that allows you to view the process without risk. Many of my colleagues believe that you cannot build wealth without risk. Let me say it another way. You cannot have prosperity without risk. Do not believe the hype.

There is an area that I believe intimidates most people. This is like a cancer to your finances. Once you create it, it seems to continue to grow and eat away at your life's savings. So, we looked at eliminating debt by cutting it out, chunks at a time. Using the financial foundation approach (budget), it was the Blair family's debt totals.

Why is this family living paycheck to paycheck each month? Where are the challenges that seem to create a shortage each month? If you recall, I asked them about their credit card debt. Mr. Blair stated that they are paying more than the minimum payment on the credit cards.

His reason for doing so is he heard that if you are making only the minimum payment you will never get out of debt. That is the type of direction and guidance that most of all the financial coaches and experts I know provide.

I do not subscribe to that type of teaching. I do accept the fact that making minimum payments only without a strategy can and will result in an endless attempt to get out of debt.

I teach strategy first. Making the minimum payment with a strategic plan of action allows you the freedom to eliminate debt and build wealth. **Action Influence.**

As you can see below, with their current payments made to reduce their debt the total of debt payments is $2,242 a month. When you add that to the household expenses total of $2,608, they only had $150 remaining from their $5,000 net income each month.

This is why they are not able to save and are living paycheck to paycheck. Some of you who are reading this book may be experiencing the same things.

Debts	Current Payments	Balances
Credit Card 1	$580.00	$14,500.00
Credit Card 2	$520.00	$11,000.00
Credit Card 3	$367.00	$5,300.00
Credit Card 4	$450.00	$11,000.00
Credit Card 5	$325.00	$8,000.00
	$2,242.00	**$49,800.00**

Once you determine that you want financial freedom, you must set goals that are relative to your family. There is a lot of information out there; most of it sounds the same.

As I mentioned in earlier chapters, knowing the difference between a poverty mentality and a wealth mentality becomes the first step to financial freedom. Every decision that you make has a cost associated with it.

This cost will either bring you closer to your financial goals or move you farther away. I know that it has been difficult. I know that you have tried and done the best that you know how.

"The first thing you learn is the hardest to unlearn. It is better to be uneducated than to be miseducated! Keep a hungry heart for truth!" -Bishop Dale C. Bronner

Now, step back. Make a commitment to make wealth conscious decisions in every action of your life. Determine the financial impact of all decisions made. Focus on providing a way of life for you and your family first. **"It doesn't matter how you start, it matters how you end! You either live by default or design!" -Bishop Dale C. Bronner**

This is what I want your foundation to do for you: secure the needs of your household and maintain a standard of living that suits you, not the Joneses. Honor your faith, enjoy activities with your family and enjoy the comfort of your home.

Next, protect that way of life for your household. Why do we do things the way that we do them? Most of the time it comes down to being driven by our emotions and fear.

Our emotions can influence financial decisions in surprisingly predictable ways. We tend to be overconfident in our own knowledge and decisions, we extrapolate recent trends while dismissing the past, and we refuse to accept losses gracefully by hanging on to them far too long, and so on.

Frequently, we make what we firmly believe to be rational decisions, but those decisions are primarily based on the input of our own emotions, not ideas, data, or analysis. Sometimes the emotional displays of people close to us affects our decision-making.

You are going to have to redefine your mission. Your purpose must be clear. It is to learn financial freedom and wealth building and to do so in a way that will influence your family for generations to come.

Action Influence

I explained to them **Action Influence**. A new paradigm shift in rediscovering your core financial desires. Understanding that the rules of wealth are steadfastness requires a complete shifting of your commitment to create wealth.

Each generation cycle is faced with this paradigm shift. Those who recognize the shift adjust and focus on creating wealth for the next generation. They see that action is required if they are to become successful. What is **Action Influence**?

Action Influence is simply taking the definition of paradigm and applying its meaning to influence your financial decision.

(**Paradigm** - A set of assumptions, concepts, values, and practices that constitutes a way of viewing reality for the community that shares them, especially in an intellectual discipline.)

You must create a **set of assumptions** for your financial life. As a result, these assumptions become the financial goals that you will set.

You must create **concepts** to implement and put your assumptions to work. These concepts are the planning practices to save, invest and eliminate debt.

You must establish your personal **values** as they relate to your assumptions and your concepts. These personal values allow you to put them in order so that you can accomplish them once they are prioritized.

By taking these actions, your daily **practice** will now **constitute** a way of life and how you review the **reality** of your financial goals. It will require discipline.

In order for **Action Influence** to become a paradigm shift for you, your mindset has to change. Most people operate under a paradigm of some kind, either by decision or by default. It is referred to as learned behavior. Any one paradigm may not necessarily be fair or right; it is measured by the required traits of its definition.

Action Influence paradigm shift is creating a framework containing all of the commonly accepted views about finance, a structure of what direction you should take and how it should be performed.

Knowing the difference between poverty and wealth and having a fundamental change in your individual views and that of society. You will need a committed practice that constitutes new discipline at a certain point in time.

Over time, the very **action** that you take in organizing your financial life as I am describing in this book will branch out into your behavior and the power that influences your ability to grow your wealth.

So many things play a major role in affecting your behavior. Therefore, you act at different times and in different places. For many, our lack of sound money skills affects our ability to manage money.

The Blairs now had to take a new action to influence their financial future in a way that affects them right away. It had to be my call to action to show them the impact that they can have on their lives. Please place yourself in the mindset of the Blair family.

They are working hard to provide and protect a way of life for their family. Their efforts seemed unrewarding more to often, they are full of disappointments, a lack of any real savings and there are things that just happen in life (water heater repair, car repair, children events).

Their debt total payments are $2,242 a month. When you add that to the household expenses total of $2,608, they only had $150 remaining from their $5,000 net income each month. Not much room here for change.

So, I ordered them to set the debt budget to minimum payments only. YES, I said minimum payments only. Mr. Blair asked me if I was out of my mind. He went on to say that every financial expert including the President has stated that making the minimum payments on a credit card is committing financial suicide.

He said, "Mr. Wilson, I am not going to put my family at risk. You talk a good game, Sir, but I do not see how making such a drastic move will protect my family."

You may have thought the same thing when you first read it. After all, there are countless stories, books and articles speaking highly against simply making the minimum payment.

His wife was once a great supporter and now she was looking at me as if I had become a great disappointment. She was my ally in this whole process. I got in a save (yourself, man) mode.

"Wait!" I said with passion. We have been at this for some hours now. Each time we hit a roadblock it was for a purpose. Let me show you what you cannot see.

Then I adjusted the current payments to the minimum payments and asked them to take a look now. They saw these adjustments.

Debts	Minimum Payments	Balances
Credit Card 1	$280.00	$14,500.00
Credit Card 2	$220.00	$11,000.00
Credit Card 3	$167.00	$5,300.00
Credit Card 4	$100.00	$11,000.00
Credit Card 5	$125.00	$8,000.00
	$892.00	**$49,800.00**

They now see that their remaining income after paying all of their bills is now 10 times what they previously had each month. Yes, the new remaining income is now $1,500 each month.

It was a DUH moment. I redeemed myself only for a moment. Mr. Blair asked, "What do we do about the debt?" That was a legitimate question.

I said to him, now we begin to focus on creating wealth. This is where **Action Influence** becomes the tool to create the wealth mentality that I have been talking about. In that next chapter, I showed them (you) how to eliminate all $49,800 dollars of debt and created the foundation to build wealth.

Having your financial foundation (budget) complete, it is now ready for you to begin to use it and get a good feel for how it can keep your finances in order.

Look at is this way. If there was not any debt at all, the only thing you have is your living and household expenses each month. What is that cost?

Think about it, your financial foundation (budget) consists of everything that runs your home, secure your family and provide a way of life. The Blair family's household expenses are $2,603 every month. It provides them with entertainment, clothes, club fees, personal care, food, car repair and insurance.

This is after the home expenses are secured and long-term savings are in place also. Imagine this is your family with the same income and no debts at all imagine the financial security you would have.

The fact that your financial foundation (budget) allows you to prepare for the future also allows you to forecast how much money you will be able to save for important things like your retirement. It is not about I deserve this or even that you have earned it.

Now dealing with their debt situation is heavily on Mr. Blair's mind, as it should be. This is where **Action Influence** really shows up and delivers. We have over $49,800 of credit card debt to eliminate.

There are things that I want you to consider before I walk you through the process that I want you to use. First, there are things that we did not concern ourselves with at all:

We did not consider:

Balances.
Interest Rate.
Type of credit cards.

They were not told the following:

Cut up the credit cards
Cut back on expenses
Commit to using your "raise" to paying off debt.
Contact creditors and negotiate lower rates

Use eBay to sell stuff around the house
Post your debt free goal on the fridge.
Get a part time job

I know these are things you have heard before. For years, most of my colleagues have used this approach and they are firm with this advice. I am approaching this completely different using what I believe is a stronger approach.

All of those things are important, necessary and possibly affective when your only goal is to become debt free. Being debt free is not a part of our focus. In fact, time was our focus. It was what we needed to accomplish our overall goal.

Okay, we know that there is $1,500 of remaining income. However, I am only going to show you what we did with only $700. The other $800 we will come back to later. Now, I want to deal with the debt.

Let's look at their debts again below:

Debts	Minimum Payments	Balances
Credit Card 1	$280.00	$14,500.00
Credit Card 2	$220.00	$11,000.00
Credit Card 3	$167.00	$5,300.00
Credit Card 4	$100.00	$11,000.00
Credit Card 5	$125.00	$8,000.00
	$892.00	**$49,800.00**

The very first thing that I had to make clear to them is that when we/you create this plan today, it must be complete and have a final date.

Just like you plan a fun vacation, you know when the flight leaves and return, you know where you are staying and you know how much spending money you will have.

140

This is a retirement fund planning party. You are going to know your debt elimination date, your saving and investment dates and most of all how much wealth you would have accumulated.

How is it possible that most people who struggle financially seem to have details on how to make ends meet? They are diligent in pursuing things that seem to keep them behind or deeper in debt.

Well, let's get started with the debt elimination process. As I mentioned before, the Blair family's household budget is set in stone. Their lifestyle is committed to the financial foundation (budget) that was set for them. All of their expenses have been identified and the appropriate amount is established.

With the $700 that they have committed to eliminate debt, a plan of action was created. We determined that the money to pay off debt would be saved each month as they continue to make regular minimum monthly payments on their debts.

One thing to remember is the fact that each payment towards the debt in the budget reduces the total amount owed.

Debts	Minimum Payments	Balances
Credit Card 1	$280.00	$14,500.00
Credit Card 2	$220.00	$11,000.00
Credit Card 3	$167.00	$5,300.00
Credit Card 4	$100.00	$11,000.00
Credit Card 5	$125.00	$8,000.00
	$892.00	**$49,800.00**

The debts above are the debts they will eliminate over the next 44 months. There are five steps to this and each of them requires time. They first determined the foundation of the plan of action to eliminate the debt. Mr. Blair asked how we are going to pay off this amount of debt in just 44 months.

The process will still be the same regardless of the amount of debt or remaining income. I took 46% of the remaining income to start this process.

So, regardless of your remaining income always use between 40% - 48% of that amount. This will give you an adequate amount of resources to do other things later. Refer back to Chapter 5.

Preserving your way of life requires you to evaluate the reason that you must save. It is not optional, saving is and should be an absolute part of your daily life. This is the reason that most people are very disappointing to me as a financial coach.

Most people need very little motivation to save for items that add no financial value to their homes or their lives. I remember when a desktop computer costed $1,000, one of my clients told how they saved for six months to purchase one. They were justifying that they knew how to save money. Yet, there was only $50 in their savings account some six months later.

Many financial experts agree that consumers should aim to have three to six months of living expenses saved for emergencies. They strongly believe that saving money is the cornerstone of paying for future financial goals.

142

These financial goals change as you move through life. It could be buying a home, buying a car, your college education or your children's college education.

People often feel as if they are under so much pressure to save money. They hear that there are so many of reasons to begin saving money.

Because of such pressure, people save for different reasons. Amazingly, those reasons are short-term and do not provide the resources that it was intended. There are plenty of reasons why people choose to save. I have listed eight of the most common:

Save for a New Car or Vacation
Save for a Down Payment on a House
Save for Luxury Items
Save for Emergency Funds
Save for Sinking Funds
Save for Education or for Retirement

For now, let me focus on saving this money. Mrs. Blair was nervous about this next process. It is not clear to her what I am asking them to do now.

Remember, in her eyes she sees $800 that she can do some things with. Is it funny that she can see this money now, but could not see it before I rearranged her finances?

You will have this same experience; you will put your numbers down as they are. Then, you will refocus with a plan of **Action Influence** and identify income that you should save.

Remember, "It is simply about learning how all of **your eggs in one basket** can make a difference in building wealth."

When I talk about putting all of your eggs into one basket, many of my colleagues get upset. This is something that they teach against and most people firmly believe that we should not have all of our eggs in one basket.

This is why a paradigm shift is required to accomplish the wealth accumulation desired. Let's explore just some of the reasons they teach this bad concept.

Are you putting all of your eggs in one basket?

• Do you have all of your money in the stock market?
• Do you have all of your money in your savings account?
• Do you have all of your money in fixed-income investments?

If you answered, "yes" to any of these questions, you are seriously endangering your financial health. A smart financial plan starts with diversification—allocating your assets among several investment classes.

For example, after gauging your risk tolerance you should distribute your savings among high-risk investments such as stocks, low-risk investments such as bonds and liquid investment such as money market accounts. Diversity is the key to protecting your savings. **THIS IS WHAT THEY TEACH. Refer back to Chapter 6.**

Now that the debt elimination plan is created, it is time to establish a plan for saving. The purpose is to preserve the way of life for your family. The Blair family had $200 going into their savings each month as a part of the financial foundation (budget).

It is important for them to identify this savings as long-term savings. By having the long-term savings, they are learning to expect the unexpected. This prevents a minor financial setback from turning into a major financial crisis.

That alone is not enough. With the remaining $800, I instructed them to do a number of things that made them feel comfortable. First, I divided the $800 into 4 parts, $200 going to long-term savings giving it a total of $400 a month.

I suggested they both needed to create a savings account and place $200 in each account each month. That means that both Mr. Blair and Mrs. Blair would open individual savings accounts. They had to place the final $200 into a household savings account that would serve as medium to long-term savings.

Mr. Blair was quick to point out that they may find themselves going into those savings accounts from time to time. I immediately asked him if he would really need too.
Did you not account for entertainment, personal care, clothes, gas and food in your financial foundation (budget)? What will you need this money to do?

This will be a challenge if there is not a shift in thinking. The whole purpose of creating a financial foundation (budget) is to secure life. I had to take them back to the beginning of the process and remind them that they were making debt payments with this money.

Mrs. Blair asked, "What is the plan with this money? Are we to just save it?" She asked that question as if saving money is a waste of time.

You are going to have to be very careful not to lose track of your goals. **Action Influence**, I cannot say that enough. I had to work quickly to show them the plan with this money. Refer back to Chapter 6.

Their focus had been on paying off their debt more than retirement. Does that sound familiar to you? Knowing that they now have a good solid savings plan in place, it is important to consider a solid investment plan for long-term (retirement).

Both Mr. & Mrs. Blair started talking about their 401k plans that they have on their jobs. It was a very intense conversation. They, like most households, believe that 401k investments are enough to fund your retirement. I had to make the case that it is not.

With both of them over the age of 40 and having not really started to save for retirement, making large annual contributions may not be enough to reach their retirement goals.

When you consider retirement saving and investing, there are things that you need to determine.

How much can you expect from Social Security?
What other sources of income can you count on in retirement?
How much does your employer contribute to your 401k plan?
How much are you contributing to your 401k plan?
What kind of lifestyle do you want in retirement?

All of the above questions are critical in determining how much money you will need in retirement. Do not think your 401k plan alone will be enough.

This is why we are putting together this financial plan. So, regardless of your age, do not simply rely on your 401k plan alone. I am going to talk later about 401k and your advantages.

They had purchased a $5,000 Roth Individual Retirement Account (IRA) three years ago. However, it was not making them any money. I laughed, then told them that based on the budget information and all of the numbers that we went over, there was never any mention of monthly contributions being made to the ROTH.

Always remember that without simply making regular contributions to your IRA, the account will have minimum growth. Just a single lump-sum investment is not the answer. **Do not get trapped here.**

Listen, as I stated, they are not alone. Most people try to do something about their financial future. They will make the minimum contribution to their 401k, they will open up a Roth or some other type of investment product.
This gives them the feeling or the gratitude that they are doing something. Never consider or settle with the idea that you are trying or doing something. That is the biggest roadblock for many.

I am walking you through **Action Influence** from the beginning to your retirement. Each phase or step is necessary. Mindset, behavior, action, consciousness, thought, and influence, all affect your money and your future.

147

Now that the Blair family has identified their income, they have set a workable budget for their household with long-term (retirement) savings included in that budget, debt reduction and personal and investment savings in place. It is time to secure retirement.

We included additional money to long-term savings in their household budget. Once the budget and debt reduction was set, we increased the long-term savings from $200 to $400 a month. That became the overall long-term savings that totaled $17,600. (Refer back to the previous chapter.)

They look at the S&P 500 (Standard and Poor 500 Index) and choose to invest $200 a month into a diversified portfolio that includes a variety of products.

During this process, it gives them dollar cost averaging as they purchase stock each month. What is dollar cost averaging?

It is a technique of buying a fixed dollar amount of a particular investment on a regular schedule, regardless of the share price. More shares are purchased when prices are low, and fewer shares are bought when prices are high.

Over this period eventually, the average cost per share will become smaller and smaller. Dollar-cost averaging lessens the risk of investing a large amount in a single investment at the wrong time.
The choice of using Standard & Poor 500 Index funds are available to you and would be low-cost, no-load, which are offered by many of the major mutual fund companies.

148

As far as picking which stocks to buy, or even which mutual funds to buy, the Standard and Poor 500 Index funds have reduced this to a no-brainer.

When you buy shares of a market index like a Standard and Poor 500 Index, you can expect to get the rate of return of the overall market.

With this fund, you will always be widely diversified in a broadly based cross section of the economy and should expect to prosper over the years to the same extent as our country prospers.

The investment approach, Dollar Cost Averaging, means you will regularly and automatically buy a fixed dollar amount of your fund every month or every pay period without regard to whether the price of these shares is up or down at the time you invest.

This becomes a major part of your retirement plan. This is not eliminating your 401k or any other investment or savings. This is just one more ingredient for the master retirement plan. Once you follow each of these steps, you are well on your way.

Remember **"Controlling your savings and investing creates the environment that your spending is choked off. - Rob Wilson"**

This is how you are going to define your own purpose to financial security. Financial security is an admirable goal, the **Action Influence** that you take makes it achievable.

149

A Motivational Quote

In life, friendships change...divorces happen...people move on and others die. Money and jobs will come and go. Live long enough and your health and body will change. It goes with the territory of being human.

The fact that you are still here gives you an advantage. Do not look back. Look straight ahead! Decide to use all of your knowledge, skills, experiences, as well as your life lessons from your mistakes, defeats and setbacks, to start over again.

Life changes. You may not have the same life as before, but you can still enjoy your life! You have GREATNESS within you!

- Les Brown is a dynamic personality and highly-sought-after renowned motivational speaker.

Chapter 10

Your Ability to Save
The Awesome (WIN) Power

According to the U.S. Consumer Savings and Debt Report, it appears consumers are returning to their old spending habits after being exposed by their bad savings habits in the recent 2008 financial crisis.

While spending can be a sign of economic recovery, there must be a greater effort to save for your financial security. Otherwise, everything you just read simply means nothing towards financial freedom.

This is where **Action Influence** will make a huge difference by changing the way you are saving money. There needs to be a designed purpose to help encourage you to manage your spending and savings increase in tandem with not incurring additional liabilities.

Action Influence allows you to really see all of the benefits of saving money. By observing patterns in your own life when it comes to handling money, your financial decisions are sharper. Here is one of my personal quotes: **"Controlling your savings and investing creates the environment that your spending is choked off."**

This is true when we are faced with the idea that we have money to spend. We often feel the greater need is to pay down our debts. Yet the process of using credit cards allows us to feel that we are spending other people's money.

Everyone knows they should be saving money somewhere or somehow. We even look for different ways to save. Knowing your ability to save money will be the cornerstone of building wealth.

Depending upon your needs, lifestyle preferences and income, the amount of money you are able to save will be different from that of your friends, family and neighbors.

Earlier in the book, I wrote about how money begets money. This is a fundamental principle of finance. One of which is the concept of $1 saved or invested today is more valuable than $1 a year from now. We've talked about the time value of money. This concept can begin in the simplest form.

I want to caution you. Many feel that due to their hard work and the stress of life they deserve to enjoy small luxury items.

This idea is entirely personal and should be challenged with caution. Learning the concept of time value of money and how a $10 savings will grow over time is the cornerstone.

It really comes down to understanding **"Simple processes create great moments."** Every small luxury item that you think nothing of can cost you millions of dollars in future wealth.

This entire book is about helping you to see how **Action Influence** and a paradigm shift will create value concepts.

If you firmly establish the time value of money concept in your head, you will create wealth. A key to financial prosperity is realizing the potential value of every dollar that comes into your hands.

In fact, remembering every decision that you make will bring you closer to your financial dreams or move you further away. Every decision has a cost associated with it. Money is like a seed or an egg.

They both have the ability to be consumed or to reproduce. If you only see your money as a seed, you may simply consume it and it is forever gone. However, if you decided to sow it or save it, it will reproduce new money over time.

Never settle with the idea that you will make or earn more money. It's every single dollar that will give you a chance to create wealth.

With the egg, you again have the ability to consume it. However, if you decide to hatch it, it will produce a chicken that will produce more eggs. The process as with money is also built on the concept of time value.

The requirement or commitment to save money is often easier said than done. With a true budget or financial foundation you will find plenty of ways to help you begin saving money.

I have designed three simple saving concepts to get you
started. With Savings Plan One you only save the amount of
money based upon the number of the weeks in the year. It
allows individuals with limited income to start small and
build up their savings.

Action Influence Savings Plan 1

Week Number	Save This Amount	Your Total	Week Number	Save This Amount	Your Total
1	$ 1.00	$ 1.00	27	$ 27.00	$ 378.00
2	$ 2.00	$ 3.00	28	$ 28.00	$ 406.00
3	$ 3.00	$ 6.00	29	$ 29.00	$ 435.00
4	$ 4.00	$ 10.00	30	$ 30.00	$ 465.00
5	$ 5.00	$ 15.00	31	$ 31.00	$ 496.00
6	$ 6.00	$ 21.00	32	$ 32.00	$ 528.00
7	$ 7.00	$ 28.00	33	$ 33.00	$ 561.00
8	$ 8.00	$ 36.00	34	$ 34.00	$ 595.00
9	$ 9.00	$ 45.00	35	$ 35.00	$ 630.00
10	$ 10.00	$ 55.00	36	$ 36.00	$ 666.00
11	$ 11.00	$ 66.00	37	$ 37.00	$ 703.00
12	$ 12.00	$ 78.00	38	$ 38.00	$ 741.00
13	$ 13.00	$ 91.00	39	$ 39.00	$ 780.00
14	$ 14.00	$ 105.00	40	$ 40.00	$ 820.00
15	$ 15.00	$ 120.00	41	$ 41.00	$ 861.00
16	$ 16.00	$ 136.00	42	$ 42.00	$ 903.00
17	$ 17.00	$ 153.00	43	$ 43.00	$ 946.00
18	$ 18.00	$ 171.00	44	$ 44.00	$ 990.00
19	$ 19.00	$ 190.00	45	$ 45.00	$ 1,035.00
20	$ 20.00	$ 210.00	46	$ 46.00	$ 1,081.00
21	$ 21.00	$ 231.00	47	$ 47.00	$ 1,128.00
22	$ 22.00	$ 253.00	48	$ 48.00	$ 1,176.00
23	$ 23.00	$ 276.00	49	$ 49.00	$ 1,225.00
24	$ 24.00	$ 300.00	50	$ 50.00	$ 1,275.00
25	$ 25.00	$ 325.00	51	$ 51.00	$ 1,326.00
26	$ 26.00	$ 351.00	52	$ 52.00	$ 1,378.00

Next, is Savings Plan Two. We all can agree that over the course of our daily lives we waste at least $20 a week. This plan allows you to now save less than that to begin the process of building your savings.

Action Influence Savings Plan 2

Week Number	Save This Amount	Your Total	Week Number	Save This Amount	Your Total
1	$19.76	$19.76	27	$19.76	$533.52
2	$19.76	$39.52	28	$19.76	$553.28
3	$19.76	$59.28	29	$19.76	$573.04
4	$19.76	$79.04	30	$19.76	$592.80
5	$19.76	$98.80	31	$19.76	$612.56
6	$19.76	$118.56	32	$19.76	$632.32
7	$19.76	$138.32	33	$19.76	$652.08
8	$19.76	$158.08	34	$19.76	$671.84
9	$19.76	$177.84	35	$19.76	$691.60
10	$19.76	$197.60	36	$19.76	$711.36
11	$19.76	$217.36	37	$19.76	$731.12
12	$19.76	$237.12	38	$19.76	$750.88
13	$19.76	$256.88	39	$19.76	$770.64
14	$19.76	$276.64	40	$19.76	$790.40
15	$19.76	$296.40	41	$19.76	$810.16
16	$19.76	$316.16	42	$19.76	$829.92
17	$19.76	$335.92	43	$19.76	$849.68
18	$19.76	$355.68	44	$19.76	$869.44
19	$19.76	$375.44	45	$19.76	$889.20
20	$19.76	$395.20	46	$19.76	$908.96
21	$19.76	$414.96	47	$19.76	$928.72
22	$19.76	$434.72	48	$19.76	$948.48
23	$19.76	$454.48	49	$19.76	$968.24
24	$19.76	$474.24	50	$19.76	$988.00
25	$19.76	$494.00	51	$19.76	$1,007.76
26	$19.76	$513.76	52	$19.76	$1,027.52

Our daily savings plans allows you to determine how much a day you would like to save each month. Based upon the number of days in that month, you would save the amount shown.

This is designed for an individual that has income that will allow them to maintain this pace. A great example of this is a person that earns daily tips. A simple $5 a day tip allows you to save over $1,800 a year.

Action Influence Savings Plan 3

Month	No of Days	$3 A Day	$4 A Day
January	31	$ 93.00	$ 124.00
February	28	$ 84.00	$ 112.00
March	31	$ 93.00	$ 124.00
April	30	$ 90.00	$ 120.00
May	31	$ 93.00	$ 124.00
June	30	$ 90.00	$ 120.00
July	31	$ 93.00	$ 124.00
August	31	$ 93.00	$ 124.00
September	30	$ 90.00	$ 120.00
October	31	$ 93.00	$ 124.00
November	30	$ 90.00	$ 120.00
December	31	$ 93.00	$ 124.00
Total Amount Saved		$ 1,095.00	$ 1,460.00

Month	No of Days	$5 A Day	$6 A Day	$7 A Day
January	31	$ 155.00	$ 186.00	$ 217.00
February	28	$ 140.00	$ 168.00	$ 196.00
March	31	$ 155.00	$ 186.00	$ 217.00
April	30	$ 150.00	$ 180.00	$ 210.00
May	31	$ 155.00	$ 186.00	$ 217.00
June	30	$ 150.00	$ 180.00	$ 210.00
July	31	$ 155.00	$ 186.00	$ 217.00
August	31	$ 155.00	$ 186.00	$ 217.00
September	30	$ 150.00	$ 180.00	$ 210.00
October	31	$ 155.00	$ 186.00	$ 217.00
November	30	$ 150.00	$ 180.00	$ 210.00
December	31	$ 155.00	$ 186.00	$ 217.00
Total Amount Saved		$ 1,825.00	$ 2,190.00	$2,555.00

These savings plans are very simple and can be used as a platform of building the foundation of saving. Once you have created your budget, the numbers with these plans can really increase and your wealth accumulation process is well on the way.

It will be a horrible mistake to compare yourself with others when it comes down to your financial goals. Move away from the concept of having only six months of savings.

Your financial goals are much larger than preparing for a job lay off, unemployment and even sickness. The goals that you set should look beyond your lifetime or at the very least your retirement years.

Never sacrifice the opportunity to save money in order to pay off debt. When you pay off a debt, mainly credit cards or unsecured debt, it is as if you have taken your money out to the backyard and burned it. So, as I previously discussed, all debt reduction should be matched equally with savings.

Remember, as you work to increase your financial security and build wealth, milestones make your goals attainable but **Action Influence** becomes the motivating fuel that carries you from growth to growth.

Realizing that your assumptions, concepts and goals give you motivation to focus, applying **Action Influence** in setting your goals is critical.

When you take control of your financial life, you must set personal and retirement goals. **Action Influence** will also require you to consult resources to provide you more inspiration.

Get your household involved in your saving goals. Your total environment must be supportive. You will need to celebrate wins as you reach the various milestones.

A client came to me as I was writing this book to celebrate reaching $50,000 saved. They were so encouraged about being able to reach the milestone in a reasonable time frame, that they decided to save even more.

For reaching that goal the sweet reward was to continue to save and plan for a mini vacation.

A journey should always contain a few vital elements. First, there should be a true desire to go on the journey. Secondly, a sense of knowing where you are going. Finally, a defined purpose of the journey.

When you know that the season is right to real financial change in your life, determine the elements that are required. Wealth, abundance, financial freedom, a debt-free life and serenity requires a journey to travel. Prepare well.

It will be a mistake to compare yourself to others. Your ability to save is different from others, so always pursue things appropriate for your situation. The best starting point is to gauge whether your expectations and assumptions are reasonable.

Final Words: We are an optimistic lot, except when it comes to one thing – our ability to *save money*. If we had a better grasp of how effective a simple savings plan can be, if we understood the true power of compound interest and appreciated the true value of time, I'm sure more of us would try to save.

A Motivational Quote

"You can start over again! Do not even think about quitting now! It is easy to replay in your mind how things did not work; how much you've lost; what you're going through; and how angry you are. There is no amount of conversation or magic that is going to wipe the slate clean."

You are wasting valuable time and energy that could be used to regain a new normal and start another version of your life. Even though you are hurt and you may be feeling down ~ stop kicking yourself! Face what has happened and make the decision to start over again. You have GREATNESS within you!

- Les Brown is a dynamic personality and highly-sought-after renowned motivational speaker.

What you should have learned in this chapter:

1. To manage your spending and savings increase in tandem without incurring additional liabilities.
2. Knowing your ability to save money will be the cornerstone of building wealth.
3. Your needs, lifestyle preferences,income and the amount of money you are able to save will be different from your friends, family and neighbors.
4. A dollar saved or invested today is more valuable than a dollar a year from now.
5. Every small luxury item you think nothing of can cost you millions of dollars in future wealth.
6. A key to financial prosperity is realizing the potential value of every dollar that comes into your hands.
7. Never settle with the idea that you will make or earn more money.
8. Every single dollar will give you a chance to create wealth.
9. Never sacrifice the opportunity to save money in order to pay off debt.
10. Understand the true power of compound interest and appreciate the true value of time

Chapter 11

Certificates of Deposit –
The Awesome (WIN) Power

Once you become committed to saving, you will have to look beyond just a regular checking and savings account. There are some saving and investing steps I want you to consider.

First, I want you to look at and research relatively low-risk investments that can easily be converted into cash. A certificate of deposit (CD) is a special type of deposit account.

Bank or credit union CDs typically offer higher rates of interest than regular savings accounts. Unlike other investments, CDs feature federal deposit insurance up to $250,000.

This is how CDs can work for you: When you purchase a CD, you invest a fixed sum of money for a fixed period of time—six months, one year, five years, or more—and in exchange, the issuing bank pays you interest, typically at regular intervals.

When you cash in or redeem your CD, you receive the money you originally invested plus any accrued interest. But if you redeem your CD before it matures, you may have to pay an "early withdrawal" penalty or forfeit a portion of the interest you earned.

There are two main factors that affect bank CD rates available to you.

They are:
The length of time until the CD matures, and
The current interest rate environment

The longer you'll have your money tied up, the higher your rate will be. Check around, you'll find that bank CD rates go up as the length of time increases.

This is because the longer you commit to leaving your money, the more flexibility the bank has with your money. They are willing to pay you a better rate because they can use the money for a wider variety of purposes.

Current interest rates are also an important factor. That is because bank CD rates are set according to other competitive rates out there.

The bank knows that you have a variety of choices, so you'll find that banks try to stay competitive when setting rates. Pay attention over the coming years. If you see interest rates rising, you'll also see bank CD rates rising.

Other factors can influence bank CD rates. For example, you will find that a bank is trying to win some short-term business by offering slightly higher rates. They know that there

Certificates of Deposit - The Awesome (WIN) Power

are people out there shopping bank CD rates, and they hope that once they get a customer in the door the customer will stay (and bring over additional assets).

Another factor is the desired profitability. You may find that credit unions have rates that are slightly higher than bank CD rates. Because credit unions are nonprofits, they can afford to offer a little more to the customer at the expense of reaping higher margins.

Although most investors have traditionally purchased CDs through local banks, many brokerage firms now offer CDs.

These brokerage firms—known as "deposit brokers"—can sometimes negotiate a higher rate of interest for a CD by promising to bring a certain amount of deposits to the institution. The deposit broker can then offer these "brokered CDs" to their customers.

At one time, most CDs paid a fixed interest rate until they reached maturity. But, like many other products in today's markets, CDs have become more complicated. Investors may now choose among variable rate CDs, long-term CDs, and CDs with special redemption features in the event the owner dies.

Some long-term, high-yield CDs have "call" features, meaning that the issuing bank may choose to terminate (or call) the CD after only one year or some other fixed period of time.

Only the issuing bank may call a CD, not the investor. For example, a bank might decide to call its high-yield CDs if interest rates fall.

But if you've invested in a long-term CD and interest rates subsequently rise, you'll be locked in at the lower rate. Before you consider purchasing a CD from your bank or brokerage firm, make sure you fully understand all of its terms.

Carefully read the disclosure statements, including any fine print. Don't be dazzled by high yields. Ask questions and demand answers before you invest. These are my tips that can help you assess what features make sense for you:

Find out when the CD matures. As simple as this sounds, many investors fail to confirm the maturity dates for their CDs and are later shocked to learn that they've tied up their money for five, ten, or even twenty years. Before you purchase a CD, ask to see the maturity date in writing.

For brokered CDs, identify the issuer. Federal deposit insurance is limited to a total aggregate amount of $250,000 for each depositor in each bank or thrift institution, it is very important that you know which bank or thrift issued your CD.

In other words, find out where the deposit broker plans to deposit your money. Also be sure to ask what record-keeping procedures the deposit broker has in place to assure your CD will have federal deposit insurance.

For more information about federal deposit insurance, read the FDIC's publication, Your Insured Deposits, or call the FDIC's Central Call Center at (877) 275-3342 or (877) ASK-FDIC. For the hearing impaired call 1-800-925-4618 or 1-202-942-3147 in Washington, D.C.

Certificates of Deposit - The Awesome (WIN) Power

Investigate any call features. Callable CDs give the issuing bank the right to terminate the CD after a set period of time but they do not give you that same right. If the bank calls or redeems your CD, you should receive the full amount of your original deposit plus any unpaid accrued interest.

Understand the difference between call features and maturity. Don't assume that a "federally insured one-year non-callable" CD matures in one year. If you have any doubt, ask the sales representative at your bank or brokerage firm to explain the CD's call features and to confirm when it matures.

Confirm the interest rate you'll receive and how you'll be paid. You should receive a disclosure document that tells you the interest rate on your CD and whether the rate is fixed or variable. Be sure to ask how often the bank pays interest – for example, monthly or semi-annually. And confirm how you'll be paid—for example, by check or by an electronic transfer of funds.

Ask whether the interest rate ever changes. If you're considering investing in a variable-rate CD, make sure you understand when and how the rate can change. Some variable-rate CDs feature a "multi-step" or "bonus rate" structure in which interest rates increase or decrease over time according to a pre-set schedule.

Other variable-rate CDs pay interest rates that track the performance of a specified market index, such as the S&P 500 or the Dow Jones Industrial Average.

Research any penalties for early withdrawal. Be sure to find out how much you'll have to pay if you cash in your CD before maturity.

Ask whether your broker can sell your CD. Some brokered CDs are issued in the name of the "custodian" or deposit brokers. In some cases, the deposit broker may advertise that the CD does not have a prepayment penalty for early withdrawal.

In those cases, the deposit broker will instead try to resell the CD for you if you want to redeem it before maturity. If interest rates have fallen since you purchased your CD and demand is high, you may be able to sell the CD for a profit.

But if interest rates have risen, there may be less demand for your lower-yielding CD. That means you may have to sell the CD at a discount and lose some of your original deposit.

Visit credit unions. A recent survey by www.Bankrate.com shows once again that credit unions offer higher interest than banks and thrifts on share certificates (also known as certificates of deposit).

The interest advantage is often better than a half-percent. The Bankrate.com survey states that six-month credit union share certificates had a higher national average yield.

Certificates of Deposit - The Awesome (WIN) Power

What you should have learned in this chapter:

1. Once you become committed to saving, you will have to look beyond just a regular checking and savings account.
2. Research relatively low-risk investments that can easily be converted into cash.
3. Unlike other investments, CDs feature federal deposit insurance up to $250,000.
4. CDs allow you to invest a fixed sum of money for a fixed period of time—six months, one year, five years or more.
5. When you cash in or redeem your CD, you receive the money you originally invested plus any accrued interest.
6. If you redeem your CD before it matures, you may have to pay an "early withdrawal" penalty or forfeit a portion of the interest you earned.
7. There are two main factors that affect bank CD rates available to you. They are: The length of time until the CD matures and the current interest rate environment
8. The longer you'll have your money tied up, the higher your rate will be.
9. Pay attention over the coming years. If you see interest rates rising, you'll also see bank CD rates rising.
10. You will find that a bank is trying to win some short-term business by offering slightly higher rates.
11. You may find that credit unions have rates that are slightly higher than bank CD rates.
12. Although most investors have traditionally purchased CDs through local banks, many brokerage firms now offer CDs.

13. Understand the difference between call features and maturity
14. Before you purchase a CD, ask to see the maturity date in writing.
15. A bank might decide to call its high-yield CDs if interest rates fall.
16. Don't assume that a "federally insured one-year non-callable" CD matures in one year.

Chapter 12

Your 401k - The Awesome (WIN) Power

First, let me start out by saying that as I discuss using 401k plans and processes I want to keep you in context. We are talking about your financial future, your retirement and you being in a position to provide wealth to the next generation.

In building your financial foundation, you now recognize that you will need the type of investment accounts that you just learned about in earlier reading. The needs of your family, household and life were set up with your financial foundation.

Those accounts, certificates of deposit and IRA accounts will not be enough for your retirement needs. This is the compelling reason for directing money to all of these accounts, rather than concentrating your efforts on just a 401k plan.

My research has shown that people fall into one of three areas regarding 401k plans. The first group chooses not to invest right away into a 401k plan because they do not understand it or they feel that they cannot afford it.

That next group will make an investment into a 401k plan, but will only do a minimum contribution that will not meet the company's match. Again, it is the fear that they need this money now and will not invest more.

Finally, the last group will invest the minimum to meet the company's match, but they will not consider anything outside of that investment. At this point, you should recognize that there is a need to create multiple savings and investment components.

The goal here is to change your mindset and to give you control. In the first two chapters, I challenged you to understand and commit to establishing and following a master plan that will bring you financial freedom.

You must move financial independence to the top of your financial priority list. You should make it number one in your financial life, and make everything else secondary.

Clearly, you have heard that there are many reasons to take advantage of the special benefits of a 401k. However, the fact remains that the money you direct to these accounts will not be available to you, for the most part, until retirement.

Please commit to your retirement future when using the investment. So many people have used this money the wrong way and have lived to regret it. I do not want you to have that experience.

At this point, I want to remind you that this is not where you go for money to make a down payment on a home, for college expenses for yourselves or your kids, for wedding expenses or whatever else may seem desirable.

Your 401k - The Awesome (WIN) Power

We discussed that already, this is where your **Action Influence** must take control.

Never use 401k to pay off credit cards.
Never use 401k or Credit Card for down payment on house.
Never use 401k money to get on your feet.
Never use 401k loan to pay off an auto loan.

Whenever there is no paradigm shift (**Action Influence**) that poverty mentality kicks in and every emergency takes precedence over building wealth. You have seen what happens when you fly by the seat of your pants.

You have tried saving money every month, then the car needs to be repaired or a special event is going on. So, you fail to save and start attacking your savings account and your entire wealth accumulation program goes nowhere fast.

That is *re-active* not **Action Influence** money management; you are responding to needs as they develop. Rather than working towards a long-term goal, you are reacting to events as they occur.

In previous chapters throughout this book, I have attempted to show you the disadvantages of this form of money management (Poverty Mentality vs. Wealth Mentality).

Your 401k retirement account will have terrific built-in tax advantages that your regular money account won't have. Your money goes into your 401k on a pre-tax basis, which gives you a tax advantage right from the start.

171

Your money will grow tax-deferred until you actually take it out. You will not be able to access this money easily until you're 59½ years old or more.

Many companies' 401k plan, may also "match" all or part of your investment, which also goes in pre-tax and provides you with even more tax-free appreciation.

When you work for a private employer, chances are good that your 401k is your major source of retirement savings.

Unlike other retirement plans, such as Individual Retirement Accounts, your 401k plans provide very generous contribution limits.

These limits are set and reviewed by The Internal Revenue Service (IRS) on an annual basis, and makes changes as they see fit.

The current limit has been in the same ballpark for a number of years, and the IRS has not raised it due to low inflation and other factors.

Before planning your 401k contribution strategy for 2013, be aware that the standard contribution limit for a 401k plan is $17,500.

If you are 50 years of age or older and are just realizing that you may be ill-prepared for retirement, research the current provision and be aware that the IRS has created a catch-up provision for 401k plans and IRA accounts.

Because of your age, you are allowed to contribute an extra $5,500 to your 401k plans in 2013 (and $1,000 extra to an

Your 401k - The Awesome (WIN) Power

IRA). Remember, the IRS is likely to raise the contribution limit at some point, so it is wise to check the limit before planning your strategy.

Due to recent years of low inflation and other factors not all employers allow these catch-up contributions, so it's always wise to check with your company before making your investment plans. Not all employers provide matching contributions. There are areas that you are not going to control.

So, how do you make your 401k program work for you? Simply consider the rules and guidelines as your first step of making a commitment. As I have stated earlier the limit set for 2013 is $17,500 for 401k contributions.

Some employers limit the percentage of an employee's paycheck that can be contributed to the 401k, so you might not be able to contribute that much.

If you work for an employer that set a cap for 401k contributions it is a good idea to speak to your Human Resources representative about lifting that cap.

When deciding to make contributions, always be committed to a minimum of what the employer will match to capture the maximum.

Keep in mind that there are two main factors that you should be focusing on. There are the company's match and the tax advantages. This combination really shows **Action Influence** on your money.

Your employer could match your contributions from 0% to 100%, in most cases not to exceed 6% of your salary. Imagine being able to earn an immediate 50% on all of the new money that you invest every year, up to a maximum of 6% of salary? What would that look like?

If your salary was $35,000 a year, your annual contribution would be $2,100, your employer's annual contribution would be $1,050, and that would give you a total annual contribution of $3,150.

A couple of things will be happening here. For starters, your own contribution goes into the plan pre-tax, but also the company's matching contribution goes in pre-taxed, because it's tax-deferred free money. This is a great opportunity that you cannot afford to miss out on.

The tax advantages, alone, from 401ks make them extremely desirable as investment vehicles, but when combined with a company match, they are awesome!

While it's true that there are usually restrictions on this money in the form of vesting periods and how soon you can take the money out, along with that tax consequence, the fact remains that even an immediate 25% increase on your money is fantastic.

You have got to go for this kind of deal, which is why I urge you to commit to whatever it takes to capture the maximum match. Your own contribution, the company match, the dividends, interest, and capital gains distributions—everything grows tax deferred for however long you leave it in.

Your 401k - The Awesome (WIN) Power

The big disadvantage, of course, to the 401k account, is the restriction on when and how to get our money out. Uncle Sam provides his tax benefits because he wants us to leave our money alone.

Our employer provides his company match and vesting schedule because he wants to keep us around for a while. Nobody wants to let us have easy access to our 401k money, so there is a price we have to pay for getting all of the benefits.

You will be charged taxes only on money that you take out of the account, and only if and when you take it out. Since no taxes have ever been paid on any of this money, you will have to pay ordinary income rates on everything you later withdraw from your retirement account.

Many of my colleagues suggest using your 401k to finance a new business. I do not recommend that practice at all. I know starting your own business can be an excellent way to secure your financial future.

Using the funds in your 401k plan is not the best idea. Remember, retirement money will bring you added security when you are no longer able to work.

Yes, there is a loan provision in your 401k. Consider taking out a loan against the 401k balance instead of taking the money out as a lump sum.

The loan provision on your 401k lets you avoid the 10% tax penalty and ordinary income taxes that would otherwise apply.

If you use the loan provision and take out a loan against your 401k, it is important for you to understand there are some risks as well. You may be required to pay the loan back in full if you leave your current job with the 401k loan balance still outstanding.

Any withdrawal that is permitted before the age of 59½ is subject to an excise tax equal to ten percent of the amount distributed (on top of the ordinary income tax that has to be paid), including withdrawals to pay expenses due to a financial hardship.

Except to the extent the distribution does not exceed the amount allowable as a deduction under Internal Revenue Code section 213 to the employee for amounts paid during the taxable year for medical care (determined without regard to whether the employee itemizes deductions for such taxable year).

Money that is withdrawn prior to the age of 59½ typically incurs a 10% penalty tax unless a further exception applies. This penalty is on top of the "ordinary income" tax that has to be paid upon such a withdrawal.

The exceptions to the 10% penalty include: the employee's death, the employee's total and permanent disability, separation from service in or after the year the employee reached age 55.

Also, if you quit your current employer while your 401k balance is less than $5,000, you should roll it over to an IRA. This is because the old employer will not allow you to keep a balance of less than $5,000 in his 401k plan.

Your 401k - The Awesome (WIN) Power

If you quit your employer with a balance of less than $5,000, here are the steps to follow:

- Instruct your employer to make out a check to your 401k or IRA custodian for a 401k rollover.
- Never instruct your employer to make out a check directly payable to you. If you do so, your employer will withhold a 20% federal tax and remit it to the government. Furthermore, you will also face a 10% early withdrawal penalty fee if you choose this option.

In 2013 the IRS began allowing conversions of existing Traditional 401k contributions to a Roth 401k. In order to do so, an employee's company plans must offer both a Traditional and Roth option, and explicitly permit such a conversion.

Note: If you choose to do a "conversion", the money will be taxed at that time, but it will grow tax-free from that point.

Choosing the IRA option provides you with even more expenditure options to pick from; this in particular naturally means greater results. If you are considering contributing to an IRA, you are restricted to a total of $5,500 per year (or $6,500 if over age 50) based on 2013 rates no matter how many IRA accounts you have.

There are 401k plans that charge fees for administrative services, investment management services, and sometimes outside consulting services.

They can be charged to the employer, the plan participants or to the plan itself. The fees can be allocated on a per participant basis, per plan or as a percentage of the plan's assets.

A Motivational Quote

"Refuse to live a defeated life. You were born to do GREAT things! Success can be yours...regardless of your present situation or circumstances.

Tap into the discipline, the perseverance and the mindset of determination to create a new future for yourself. Affirm to yourself that no excuse is acceptable to keep you from achieving your goal.

Surround yourself with top achievers who are focused, hungry to accomplish more, experience more and to do more with their lives. Say to yourself, as you greet each new day..."I'm going to the next level. I've got GREATNESS within me!"

- Les Brown is a dynamic personality and highly-sought-after renowned motivational speaker.

Chapter 13

Individual Retirement Account
The Awesome (WIN) Power

Your money is usually yours for the taking when your employment is terminated; or if you have changed jobs, retired and have left savings in a former employer's workplace savings plan (i.e., 401k, 403(b), governmental 457(b)). There are four things you can do with it.

Any and all loans must be paid in full before you can do anything with them.

The most desirable thing you can do, under normal circumstances, is rollover your previous savings into an IRA account. With this in mind, you can possibly set up with the same people that handle your regular money account.

You would now open a new separate IRA type account with them, and roll your old money into this account. Instruct them to continue purchasing in the same manner as before with this account as well. Contributions cannot be made to a rollover IRA like they can with a contributory IRA because the money in the rollover IRA is pre-taxed money. The broker can invest both the same way.

What actually occurs in this example is that you would first contact the account manager, where you want the money to go, and set up the new IRA account. You would do the new account paperwork and also sign a "request for transfer" form, which they would forward to your old employer.

You should also contact your old employer to tell them that the form has been sent, and ask if there is anything else you need to do to authorize this transfer.

What happens next is that your old company liquidates your savings plan, converting it to cash. The cash is then forwarded to the new IRA custodian, and the new custodian purchases the funds you told them to purchase with the money they receive.

The money passes from custodian to custodian without you ever touching it and all tax benefits are preserved. You incur no tax liabilities in the process.

The big advantage of rolling your account to an IRA with the people who handle your regular money account is that you wind up investing your old savings plan money into the exact mutual fund that you want, while maintaining all the tax benefits of your old savings plan.

Presumably, the reason you chose these people for your regular money was because you thought they were the best, and offered the best mutual fund for your purposes. Now you can get to invest some of your retirement account money with them as well. The only option that you lose is the ability to make a loan on this money.

There are three other, less desirable things you can do with your old savings plan money when you change jobs. You can sometimes leave the money where it is, sometimes move it to your new employer or let your old employer write you a check. All three of these options are less attractive than rolling this money to an IRA.

Why would you want to leave your money where it is instead of rolling it to the people who hold your regular account? You have no flexibility to manage this money if you leave it where it is, and you surely should be able to find yourself in a better situation.

As to moving your old savings plan money to a new employer, it would be extremely unlikely, in my view, for your new employer to have a plan that would provide you with greater benefits than you could gain by rolling to an IRA with your regular money account sponsor. It's not impossible. It's just unlikely. The only benefit is combining pre-tax money where you can continue adding to it.

The worst thing you can do with your old savings plan money is to have your old employer send you a check. You'll be subject to full income taxes, and if you're younger than 59½ you'll be subject to the 10% penalty as well. You surely don't want to choose this option unless you have desperate needs and nowhere else to go to get the funds.

When you retire, your choice will mainly be between leaving your money with your final employer for a while or rolling it to an IRA. Ultimately, you'll want to roll it to an IRA for pretty much the same reasons that we discussed above.

Investing your savings plan money - Summary and Review

The following is a summary of the major points presented in this section about investing your savings plan money and building wealth.

1) Your savings plan is probably the best investment opportunity you'll ever have.
2) It will help you meet all sorts of needs in addition to retirement.
3) Don't even think about not participating.
4) Begin contributing immediately. Early money earns the most.
5) Set your contribution high enough to capture the maximum company match.
6) Select the most widely diversified common stock fund offered by your plan as your investment.
7) Allocate 100% of your contribution to this selection. Splitting your investment will only dilute your return.
8) Do not tinker with your plan in any way after setting things up. Do not vary your contribution or switch back and forth between investments. Leave well enough alone.
9) A typical Vanguard 401k menu of mutual funds is discussed.
10) A typical Fidelity 401k menu of mutual funds is discussed.
11) You can take withdrawals and loans if you really need the money.
12) You should move your money to an IRA when you leave, using the IRA as a 401k Alternative

Self Directed Individual Retirement Account

Let's talk first about setting up a self directed IRA as your retirement account when you have no 401k or savings plan available to you.

This involves pretty much the same procedure as if you were to set up a regular savings or money account. You select the mutual fund company that you want to deal with, which will probably be the same company that is handling your regular money account, and request another application, but this time an IRA account application.

This account will be handled separately, of course, from your other account, even though they're at the same company.

You now determine your maximum allowable annual contribution, which at the moment, is $3,000 if you're under the age of 50. If you make $50,000 a year, this will be 6% of gross income, and you should probably contribute the maximum.

If you earn more than $50,000 and want to contribute 6%, you are out of luck because $5,500 in 2013 and 2014 for those under $53,000 is all that Uncle Sam will allow you to deduct. You'll probably do well to direct the balance of your 6%, over and above $3,000, to your regular money account, to go along with your other regular contribution.

When you've determined your contribution, say $3,000, you want to arrange for 12 monthly debits from your bank account, for $250 each, to be sent to your mutual fund company for the purchase of something like an S&P 500 Index fund.

When you first set this up, be careful that your total first year allowable contribution gets in before the IRS cutoff date, which is usually April 15th of the following year. Example: You can contribute for 2013 until April 15th of 2014, and contribute for 2014 until April 15th of 2015.

Do whatever tweaking you need to do to make the first year come out right, and then you should have it easy for future years. A wonderful thing about IRAs, as opposed to 401ks, is that at least you get to pick exactly which security you want to invest in, just as you do in your regular money account.

Most likely, your IRA will be at the same company as your regular account, and invested in the same security.

You'll instruct your mutual fund company to reinvest all dividends and capital gains distributions, and the fund company will hold all monies and securities and act as custodian for your IRA. They will send you periodic reports for this account just as they do for your regular account.

You're bound by pretty much the same tax rules as a 401k as far as leaving this money alone until you're 59½ years old and as far as money being taxed in full when you take it out.

Unlike a 401k there are no loans available against your IRA, but also unlike a 401k, there is nothing to stop you from making withdrawals any time you want, providing you are willing to pay the taxes and all the applicable penalties.

You may find that you contribute to an IRA for several years, and then leave it alone for several years when you change jobs to a company with a 401k, only to resume contributions later under different circumstances.

184

This is not a problem. Your IRA has the potential to continue to grow whether you're actively contributing or not. You also gain the convenience of dealing with a single company when you have issues concerning either account.

It's a good idea to keep the rollover IRA separate from any other IRA you may have at your selected fund company. You'll want to retain the original identity of this money because there may be specific tax considerations, which apply to this account, which do not apply to your other IRAs.

For example, some company "thrift plans" allow participants to save after-tax money, as well as pre-tax money and/or meet the company match with company stock which vests in strange ways, accompanied by complex average cost calculations.

The result is that when withdrawals are made, they are not always fully taxable, but only partially taxable, unlike normal IRA withdrawals. If this account was commingled with other IRAs, these benefits would be obscured and full taxes would always have to be paid.

Unless you know for a certainty that there are no hidden differences between two IRA accounts, it's a safer bet to keep them separate and retain their original identities. This also makes it handy to keep track of what money came from where when you've accumulated several IRAs.

The other time that you'll most likely wind up with an IRA is at retirement when you roll your company accounts into a self-directed IRA.

Although your old employer may indicate that he's willing to continue to carry your 401k accounts, you don't really want to leave it there because your access to this money would be so much more limited than it would be with an IRA at a mutual fund company or brokerage house.

When you roll this money to an IRA, you preserve all of your tax benefits but open the door to all sorts of flexibility in regards to accessing your money.

As long as you're over the age of 59½ (and sometimes even when you're not), as I said earlier, you can do whatever you want with your IRA money. You can request a check anytime you need to, or you can request a regular monthly withdrawal, or both, without needing to get approval from anyone but yourself.

You'll probably end up with several IRAs by retirement time. Consider the following scenario. You work for Company A for several years, and participate in its 401k plan, which you roll to an IRA.

Then, you leave to go to work for Company B. Company B does not have a 401k plan, so you establish a second IRA and contribute to it for several years before moving to Company C. Company C does have a 401k in which you participate until you retire, and then roll this plan into a third IRA.

You now have a rollover IRA from Company A, a rollover IRA from Company C, and a regular IRA that you used while working for Company B. All three IRA accounts may be held at the same mutual fund company and may even be invested in the same fund, such as an S&P 500 Index fund.

But most likely you have (and should) keep these three IRAs separate rather than allowing them to be combined into a single account because there is often good reason to let an IRA maintain its original identity, as we have discussed.

Let's say you already have an IRA, and this IRA is held by a local bank or brokerage house, and it's invested in whatever. You may have established this account quite a while ago, before starting to participate in your company's 401k, or you may actually be contributing to this IRA right now, because you have no 401k.

How do we go about moving this IRA to a mutual fund company where we can become invested in an S&P 500 Index fund instead of what we have right now?

There are two aspects to this move, which is called a transfer of assets to a new custodian. You must close out the previous IRA by instructing the custodian to convert your assets to cash and you must arrange for the cash to then be transferred to the new custodian and invested in an S&P 500 Index fund.

This is usually done by contacting the new custodian first, setting up your new account, and signing a request for transfer of your assets, which the new custodian will forward to the old custodian as authority for the switch.

You do well to simultaneously contact the old custodian and ask if they require anything additional from you to comply with this request. You may also need to instruct them about converting the account to cash.

If your IRA was held at a brokerage house, the broker can transfer the money between mutual funds with your instruction to do so.

If you've been invested at a bank in a bank CD, you may want to wait until the CD matures before making the switch. If you're invested in stocks, at a brokerage firm, you'll have other issues to deal with as to how and when to possibly sell your stocks in preparation for the move.

Depending on the size of the account, you may decide to avoid these decisions and leave the IRA where it is. If the account is small, however, and hasn't been doing well, you may decide to "bite the bullet", convert to cash and move the IRA to your fund company.

It's also possible that your brokerage company has the ability to receive stocks into your IRA, as is the case with Vanguard and Fidelity, so that you can move your stocks over and make decisions later.

Representatives of your new custodian will be glad to offer guidance as to how to go about these transfers. They may not want to offer investment advice but they can be extremely helpful with administrative issues, and with keeping you out of trouble with the IRS.

Once you find yourself with several separate IRA's at the same mutual fund company there's a natural tendency to want to consolidate them all into a single IRA rollover account.

Before you think of doing this be sure that there are no compelling reasons to retain the original identities of each account, such as specific tax considerations.

There's really nothing wrong with having several IRAs unless fees are eating you alive. Unless you know for a certainty that there are no hidden differences between two or more IRA accounts, it's a safer bet to keep them separate.

Just an example of what you could see regarding terms and rates on CDs and IRAs

Term	Interest Rate
1 Month CD	.90% A.P.Y.
100 Day CD	5.14% A.P.Y.
6 Month CD	4.06% A.P.Y.
7 Month CD	3.42% A.P.Y.
9 Month CD	3.65% A.P.Y.
1 Year CD	5.09% A.P.Y.
15 Month CD	4.78% A.P.Y.
18 Month CD	5.73% A.P.Y.
2 Year CD	4.37% A.P.Y.
30 Month CD	4.63% A.P.Y.
3 Year CD	4.63% A.P.Y.
4 Year CD	4.58% A.P.Y.
5 Year CD	5.05% A.P.Y.

Term	Interest Rate
1 Year IRA	5.09% A.P.Y.
15 Month IRA	4.78% A.P.Y.
18 Month IRA	5.00% A.P.Y.
2 Year IRA	4.37% A.P.Y.
30 Month IRA	4.63% A.P.Y.
3 Year IRA	4.63% A.P.Y.
4 Year IRA	4.58% A.P.Y.
5 Year IRA	5.05% A.P.Y.

With Roth IRAs, the major difference is that the Roth grows tax-free and is ideal for those expecting to be in a higher tax bracket in retirement.

The Roth IRA is not tax-deductible and the holding requirements are 5 years and 59½. The Roth does not have a Required Minimum Distribution at age 70½ like the traditional IRA does.

But if you are considering contributing to an IRA, you are restricted to a total of $5,500 per year (or $6,500 if over age 50) based on 2013 rates no matter how many IRA accounts you have.

What you should have learned in this chapter:

1. Your money is usually yours for the taking when your employment is terminated or you have changed jobs or retired.
2. You must pay off a*ny and all loans before you can get it.*
3. Rollover your previous savings into an IRA account
4. Set up account with the same people that handle your regular money account.
5. Contributions cannot be made to a rollover IRA
6. The money passes from custodian to custodian without you ever touching it and all tax benefits are preserved.
7. You incur no tax liabilities in the process.
8. In the rollover IRA is pre-taxed money

9. You can lose the option and the ability to make a loan on this money.
10. You have no flexibility to manage this money if you leave it where it is.
11. The only benefit is combining pre-tax money where you can continue adding to it.
12. You can be subject to full income taxes, and if you're younger than 59½ you'll be subject to the 10% penalty as well as if you withdraw it.
13. Use a self directed IRA as your retirement account when you have no 401k or savings plan available to you.
14. You select the mutual fund company that you want to deal with.
15. If you earn more than $50,000 and want to contribute 6%, you are out of luck because $5,500 was the cap in 2013 and 2014.
16. You'll probably do well to direct the balance of your 6%, over and above $3,000, to your regular money account.
17. Be careful when you first set this up that your total first year allowable contribution gets in before the IRS cutoff date.
18. You're bound by pretty much the same tax rules as a 401k as far as leaving this money alone until you're 59½ years old
19. Unlike a 401k there are no loans available against your IRA
20. If your IRA was held at a brokerage house, the broker can transfer the money between mutual funds with your instruction to do so.
21. With Roth IRAs, the major difference is that the Roth grows tax-free and is ideal for those expecting to be in a higher tax bracket in retirement.

22. The Roth IRA is not tax-deductible and the holding requirements are 5 years and 59½.
23. The Roth does not have a Required Minimum Distribution at age 70½ like the traditional IRA does.

Chapter 14

Action Influence - Final Words

How will you reshape your thinking or your action regarding wealth? This should not be a difficult decision after reading this book.

The real question that should be asked of me is **"What was my intent when writing this book**?" Every dictionary that I have read shows that intent is defined as *"having a plan"* or *"having a purpose."*

However, intent is not ever successfully met without some other factors. The first factor I considered was *"my reason"* or *"my motive"* for writing this book.

I wanted to create the "why" that inspires and motivates the "what." Caring and protecting your family's financial future is "the what."

Why should you care how wealth in accumulated? Over your lifetime of working, considering that you begin to work at a very early age, you most likely will earn over 1.4 million dollars.

A very well respected colleague stated once that an individual would receive 1,200 paychecks averaging $1,200 a paycheck. This would be a substantial amount of money that is likely to come through your hands.

Caring and protecting for your family with this amount of resources should be simple. The ugly fact is most families and households never realize these resources.

There is an inability to recognize their ability to save or what to save to ensure a stronger financial future for their family. So my motive was to create a genuine desire in you to want to save more and know how to do it.

The next factor is *"my agenda."* I want to give you the best look at possible options that will give you the ability to W.I.N. I believe most of us carry a self-serving agenda, one that keeps us in the hamster cage spinning our wheels paycheck after paycheck; creating more and more debt and liability while taking away the ability to save and invest.

Placing savings and investment options before you and giving you a different view on how using savings and investment products becomes a shift *(a paradigm shift)* to empower you to reach the ultimate goal to W.I.N.

Finally, my intent is to influence your "*behavior*." It is your actual behavior that will demonstrate whether or not you want to pursue wealth accumulation to allow you to W.I.N.

I want your behavior to be controlled by your action to influence your financial future. When you care about your future, your family and your goals, there is a profound demonstration of your action to protect them.

Action Influence - Final Words

I want you to realize what actually creates a W.I.N. for your household. Controlling your spending and your debt accumulation is a single step towards financial freedom.

This is not new to you; you have heard these things before. What is new, is the understanding that you have real control and influence with your money.

The ultimate power to systematically create a workable savings and investment plan without putting your household at risk is powerful. Without having to reduce the quality of your life to a rice and bean environment.

Being able to enjoy your family by taking paid vacations and not worrying about how you will meet your monthly expenses.

At the end of the day, please realize, starting any new process can be a challenge. Fear will accomplish one of two things, it will prohibit you from moving forward to accomplish your dream or it will propel you to take the actions needed to accomplish your dreams.

Therefore, my answer to the question, **"What was my intent when writing this book?"** is, I want you to W.I.N.

A Motivational Quote

Be open to change. Changing your life is hard!

"It requires everything in you to move your life in a different direction. Determine to break the habits that have caused you to live a life that does not reflect the real you.

Embrace the fear of the unknown and release the need to stay stuck in your established routines. You are bigger and stronger than any habit, addiction, or circumstance.

Change ...is not the result of wishful thinking, willpower, or even intention. It will happen because of hard work, careful planning, focused energy, and feeling the pain that has kept you stuck.

Until the pain of staying the same becomes greater than the pain of change...your life will remain exactly the way it is. This new way of living requires dedication, practice, patience and pushing yourself in the right direction over and over again."

You can change your life. You can do hard!! You have something special. You have GREATNESS within you!

- Les Brown is a dynamic personality and highly-sought-after renowned motivational speaker.

Chapter 15

Glossary

Acceleration Clause - A stipulation in a loan contract stating that the entire balance becomes due immediately if other contract conditions are not met.

Accrued Interest - Interest that has been earned but not received or recorded.

Amortization - Liquidation of a debt by making payments over a set period of time, at the end of which the balance is zero.

Annuity - A series of equal payments made at regular intervals, with interest compounded at a specified rate.

Appreciation - An increase in the value or price.

Asset - Anything an individual or business owns that has commercial or exchange value.

Auto Debit - The deduction from a checking or savings account of funds that are automatically transferred to a creditor each month. Some lenders offer interest rate discounts if loan payments are set up on auto debit at the beginning of the loan.

Balance - The amount owed on a loan or credit card, or the amount in a savings or investment account.

Balance Sheet - A financial statement showing a "snapshot" of the assets, liabilities and net worth of an individual or organization on a given date.

Bankruptcy - A legal proceeding declaring that an individual is unable to pay debts. Chapters 7 and 13 of the federal bankruptcy code govern personal bankruptcy.

Beneficiary - The person designated to receive the proceeds of a life insurance policy.

Budget - An itemized summary of probable income and expenses for a given period.

Capital - Cash or other resources accumulated and available for use in producing wealth.

Cash Flow - Money coming to an individual or business less money being paid out during a given period.

Certificate of Deposit (CD) - A type of savings account that earns a fixed interest rate over a specified period of time.

Collateral - Assets pledged to secure a loan.

Common Stock - A kind of ownership in a corporation that entitles the investor to share any profits remaining after all other obligations have been met.

Compound Interest - Interest computed on the sum of the original principal and accrued interest.

Credit - The granting of money or something else of value in exchange for a promise of future repayment.

Credit Card - A plastic card from a financial services company that allows cardholders to buy goods and services on credit.

Credit Report - A loan and bill payment history, kept by a credit reporting company and used by financial institutions and other potential creditors to determine the likelihood a future debt will be repaid.

Credit Reporting Company - An organization that compiles credit information on individuals and businesses and makes it available for a fee.

Glossary

Savings Account - A service depository institutions offer whereby people can deposit their money for future use and earn interest.

Stock Option - The right to buy or sell a corporation's stock at a predetermined price or calculable formula; sometimes used as part of employee compensation.

Stockholder - A person who owns stock in a company and is eligible to share in profits and losses; same as *shareholder*.

Tax-deferred - Phrase referring to money that is not subject to income tax until it is withdrawn from an account, such as an individual retirement account or a 401k account.

Term -The period from when a loan is made until it is fully repaid.

Terms - Provisions specified in a loan agreement.

Treasury Bill - A short-term investment issued by the U.S. government for a year or less.

Treasury Bond - A government security with a term of more than 10 years; interest is paid semiannually.

Treasury Inflation-Protected Security (TIPS) - A Treasury bond or note that is tied to inflation so that the principal amount of the investment increases or decreases according to the annual inflation rate.

Treasury Note - A government security with a maturity that can range from two to 10 years; interest is paid every six months.

U.S. Savings Bond - A nontransferable, registered bond issued by the U.S. government in denominations of $50 to $10,000.